Gipsy for Jesus

9780950413631

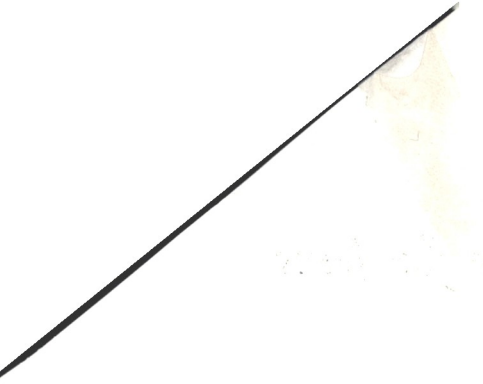

Printed by J. H. Brookes (Printers) Ltd., Hanley, Stoke-on-Trent

Gipsy for Jesus

J. B. B. FRIEND

M.O.V.E. PRESS

247, Newcastle Street, Burslem, Stoke-on-Trent

CONTENTS

CHAPTER 1

THE HOLE OF THE PIT WHENCE I WAS DIGGED
(Isa. 51.1)

MY gipsy wanderings began at a very young age, first of all as a member of "The Society of Friends", as we sometimes call our little family. A Quaker lady once asked me what right we had to the title. I told her that I felt I had earned it by quaking a lot, especially when preaching.

My mother had to bring up her two sons (there were no daughters) on a very limited income. We were, therefore, forced to live in lodgings. We managed to stay in one place for three years, from my seventh to tenth birthday. After that we were hardly ever longer than two months in any residence, if a single room could be called that. It seemed that every landlady, at the end of thirty days, felt that that was about all she could take. Unfortunately for her the law required a month's notice! Landladies appeared to our childish vision like hobgoblins with horns and tails. If the truth were told, however, I am afraid they had on their hands two impossible little rascals. A taxi driver once said to my mother, "Your children are the curse of Cape Town!" My brother was not really the culprit. He was a nice-natured, and rather gentle child (although very good at sport). I was, however, the elder by two years, and very strong-willed. Poor Geoffrey was continually being dragged into all my mischief.

Mother had high moral standards. She claimed that she had never told a lie and, as far as I can judge, this was true. My mother lectured me every time I did wrongly, and lectured me very severely. I was made to feel, and feel deeply, how disgraceful and disgusting my conduct was. But my mother never moved from words to actions. I never got the canings I so richly deserved. I, therefore, carried on with my wrongdoings, knowing that the only consequence would be a scolding. Had my father been with us I might have been a different boy, at least outwardly.

For some reason, which was not explained, my father did not live with us. He was a postmaster and did, however, always spend his annual holiday with us. On one occasion while my father was fishing, I wandered off, returning some minutes later with a fishing line. I told my father that it had apparently been abandoned and

7

that I had found it lying amongst the rocks. He seemed satisfied with that explanation until the owner turned up. That evening I was to have gone to a lantern-talk given by the famous arctic explorer, Shackelton, but my father said, "I will not take him; he has told me a lie." My mother pleaded with him. She said, "It will be of such educational value. Please take him." It was a very bitter pill to swallow, for I had wanted so much to go to that lecture, but it cured me. I never again tried to deceive my father. He, though not a religious man, had high standards, and neither drank nor smoked. He was, moreover, an old-fashioned parent, who believed in and enforced discipline. Would to God we had more of that type today.

When I was small, we never attended church, except on Good Friday and Christmas Day. Mother felt that it was right and proper to be in a place of worship on those occasions. We spent our Sundays, however, on the beach—a deserted beach, for we still had Victorian Sundays in the Cape Town of my early youth. I literally never saw a single person on a tennis-court on a Sunday, and a boy was brought before the court for kicking a football on the Sabbath. (My brother and I played football on a Sunday, but were never caught.) We must have been speckled birds, but my mother was the type who did what she wanted, though the whole world did otherwise.

We might, therefore, have grown up almost without religion, were it not for the fact that my mother, acting on a sudden impulse, stopped at an open-air meeting. Why she did so I shall never know, for my mother regarded open-air preachers as ignorant ranters. She had only been at this meeting for a few minutes when she realised that this man was a cultured gentleman, who could quote Shakespeare by the yard, and who had travelled the world as a sea-captain. At the close of his address he allowed questions. His keen intelligence, quick thinking, and rapier-like wit were more than a match for his interrogators. They were not always convinced, but certainly silenced.

In the English-speaking world of my youth there were still infidel lecturers. Their brand seems to have entirely died out. Perhaps their place has been taken by so-called "liberal Christians", who do their work of spreading doubt much more effectively. In those days, these agnostics, after having concluded their own open-air at the bottom of Adderley Street (the main thoroughfare of Cape Town), would come up to Mr. Stephens' meeting in time for the questions. As a boy I enjoyed these mental battles between the "Bible puncher" and his foes. I had no doubt as to who was the victor.

8

Later on Mr. Stephens was joined by H. W. Machan, a little man from the North of England, who was a brilliant debater and a very interesting speaker.

By that time my mother had commenced to attend the indoor meetings which were conducted by the Church of Christ, a branch of the movement started in the 18th century in the United States by Alexander Campbell under the title of "Disciples of Christ". As you would know, their main doctrine is the necessity of believers' baptism (by immersion) for salvation. The branch in Cape Town, however, held views which are not, I think, shared by other sections of this movement which has spread to many lands. For instance, they maintained that the world was flat. How a sea-captain, such as Mr. Stephens was, could subscribe to such a view, I am utterly unable to understand, but so it was. Indeed if any of us had expressed doubts as to the truth of this assertion we would have been warned that we were in grave danger of backsliding.

The women were taught "to keep silence in the churches", so that no lady ever opened her mouth in public, even in a prayer meeting. We were so taught that a "one-man ministry" was an evil, human invention that we almost regarded such ministers as agents of the Devil. We were so led to believe that we were the only body of Christians who were pleasing to God that we truly felt that to have fellowship with other professing believers would be unfaithfulness to the Lord. Yet I do honour that little church for its unshakable faith in the whole Bible as the Word of God. Once, when they were having discussions with another branch of the "Church of Christ" with a view to amalgamation, the other section complained, "There is too much of 'according to the Scriptures' with you." I believe the Lord used this attitude to create in my young heart a respect for the Bible (Isa. 66:2) and a faith in the Word of God, which has been one of the formative influences of my life.

In addition to the gipsy-career, which our lodging-life, or rather the landladies' reaction to it, forced upon us, I indulged in a private career of wandering. I was passionately fond of sport, an interest I shared with my brother, and which both of us inherited from my father. My mother encouraged this. She bought us footballs, cricket sets, tennis racquets, and arranged for us to play on one of the courts of the Y.M.C.A. But she was not prepared to allow us to play with other children. She never told us why, but I think she was afraid of their corrupting influence.

Unfortunately a game of cricket or football with my brother alone was not sufficiently interesting. I was, therefore, always running off. I would attach myself to some group, playing cricket in the summer or football in the winter. Sometimes they were boys I had never seen before, but these decent little fellows always "gave me a game", as we termed it. My mother tried to stop these wanderings. Once she left odd shoes when she had to go out. Why she did not put all the shoes away I do not know. I suppose she thought I would be too ashamed to go out with odd footwear. The pull of sport was, however, too strong, and out I slipped, a brown leather shoe on the one foot, and a light, canvas "sand shoe" on the other. Of course I could not explain to the boys, whom by the way I had not met before, the reason for my strange footwear. I, therefore, limped around, hoping that they would think that I had a sore foot, and thus needed a soft shoe. Unfortunately, in the excitement of the game, I quite forgot all about my nice little stratagem, and was running gaily round on both feet with equal fierceness. Fortunately, my fellow-players were little gentlemen, and drew no attention to my strange appearance down below.

Saturday was THE day, when all the cricket and football matches were played. Of course, as every right-thinking person fully realised, it was impossible, utterly impossible, to stop away from these all-important events. But could I make my mother understand this? "I want you to go in for sport, but why can't you be satisfied with a quiet game with your brother?" Playing a lonely, monotonous game with one little fellow, and he my brother, when I could be experiencing all the thrill and excitement of a cup-final? It was unthinkable, just unthinkable! So another stratagem was needed, and produced. As we walked along the streets I would drop behind, just a few paces at a time, so that it would not be too noticeable, until we reached a corner. There I would dart off in full speed in the opposite direction. By the time my mother discovered my absence I was safely out of reach.

I could not, of course, ask my mother for money for this forbidden pleasure. The absence of the wherewithal to purchase a ticket was, however, no problem, for the fences were ridiculously easy to climb. There was, though, another difficulty. Sometimes an official came round to make sure that all had come in via the paying-office. As I had no ticket to show I kept this gentleman carefully in view. When he was at the top of the ground I was at the bottom. When he was clipping tickets on the left I was standing in serene safety on the right side. I always won this game of hide and seek, otherwise I might have had a rather uncomfortable interview with someone in authority.

Saturday was also my cinema-night. After the football or

cricket game was over I would walk the four miles into the centre of the city, and wait for the "bioscope" (as we call the movies in South Africa) to begin. I always found a way of watching the film without paying. Then I would trudge my weary way home to an anxious mother, who for hours had been wondering about her missing, wayward boy. Once I decided to sleep in the grounds of the large boarding-house where we were staying temporarily. I had a stone for a pillow, like Jacob at Bethel. I think I felt that behaving for one night at least, like a Bible character, would be some sort of atonement for my bad behaviour during the day. I do not know how Jacob managed it, but I certainly could not sleep under those circumstances, and I finally crept softly into the one room in which we lived. My mother was so relieved to see me that I escaped that night without a scolding.

With all my other misdeeds I had acquired the smoking habit. One evening, as I was walking on the balcony of the large lodging house in which, when I was seven years of age, we were living, I saw to my pleased surprise a packet of cigarettes standing invitingly open. I continued this indulgence for several years. I suppose it was just because it made me feel grown-up, for it always produced a "sickly feeling". Once I was quite seriously ill, and my mother had to call in a doctor. He was frankly puzzled and I dared not tell him the real cause—a rather large cigar I had "found" on the dressing table of a room I had no right to enter.

The thieving habits, which had resulted from my obsession with the "seductive weed", spread unfortunately to other areas of my life, and I began to grab articles from toy counters of large stores, to run off with cricket balls from the playing grounds of schools, and even to take money from my mother's purse.

With all this, I had a vile temper, and was so untruthful that I hardly knew when I was lying or not. Yet in the midst of all my sin and shame, I continued to attend church *willingly*. My mother once said, "I cannot understand you. You run away from home. I do not know where you are, yet you always turn up for the Bible study meeting on Tuesday evenings."

You may have wondered how, with all this roaming and rushing about, my schooling was progressing. Well, the simple fact was, I had none. My mother taught me herself until I reached about the level of the last year at a primary school. By that time I was about eleven years of age, and we were staying with Jewish people. It was the time of the First World War, and difficult to get staff. The father of this family, who was the owner of a fairly large printing press, asked my mother if she would allow me to come and work in his office. My mother gladly gave permission. I think she felt that it would keep me out of mischief, which indeed it did!

I enjoyed the work, and I must have given satisfaction for they kept me on *UNTIL* one morning they sent me to the School Board with a rubber stamp, which the officials had ordered. They "smelt a rat". When I returned to the office I found a very worried owner and manager. "You must go home at once." A little later my mother and I were summoned to the School Board. One of the officials examined me to find out how much I had actually learned at home. They seemed satisfied with my answers, but made it quite clear that I would have to be sent to school immediately. They did not, however, send anyone to find out whether their instructions were being obeyed, and my mother remained adamant in her decision not to send me to a public institution of learning.

To this day, I do not know why my mother was so averse to sending me to school. I do know, however, that nothing could change this attitude. The result was that for the next two years, apart from a short period when a teacher took me for an hour or so in the afternoons, I was to have no formal education. Finally, at the beginning of 1921, when I was nearly fourteen years of age, my mother was able to place me with a private teacher. I think this lady took pity on my mother, who had a very limited income, and charged a very nominal fee for my brother's and my tuition.

Under more favourable circumstances, Miss H. would have been able to give me a better education than I could have obtained in a public school. She was an M.A. from Oxford, and an experienced teacher. Unfortunately, however, she had a desperately full programme. Looking back now, from a more mature viewpoint, I do not know how her body stood the strain. After spending the whole of each morning (apart from Saturday and Sunday) acting as governess to a wealthy family, she would come back in the early afternoon to take a long series of private classes from Continental languages (of which she seemed to know several) to art appreciation, shorthand and book-keeping. As my brother and I were kind of charity pupils, we had to be satisfied with odd moments, which she could squeeze in between the other students.

CHAPTER 2

A NAME THAT I LIVED—YET DEAD
(Rev. 3:1)

At first I was quite a keen student. I think I was tired of the aimless life I had been leading, and was sincerely glad to get some education, but, alas! my interest in Christianity was slowly, but surely, waning. Had the Lord not graciously intervened I might have lost all the little religion I had.

About June, 1921, the well-known Brethren evangelist, Fred Elliot, visited Cape Town. My mother pleaded with me to attend his meetings but, for quite a while, in vain. At long last I went. Why, I really do not know. Perhaps it was "just to get some peace". It was difficult to get me to Mr. Elliot's services but, after the first meeting, it was impossible to keep me away. Miss H. scolded me for neglecting my studies, but all to no purpose. Mr. Elliot spent several months in our city, and I followed him all over the place. Once in a crowded gathering, Mr. Elliot asked the boys and girls to sit on the platform to make room for the adults. As I passed the evangelist, he said to me, "Perhaps the Lord will make a preacher of you, my boy."

Mr. Elliot had an attractive personality. He preached the Gospel in a most winsome way, and had a very powerful gift of effective illustration. What, however, drew me most was his joy. I am afraid that I had seen little joy in the Christian circles in which I had moved. My heart hungered to know the gladness the evangelist so evidently experienced and, more than once, I longed to raise my hand in response to Mr. Elliot's appeal. I was, however, desperately shy and, time after time, my courage failed me.

At Mr. Elliot's meetings, however, we contacted a Mr. T., or rather he approached us. He was thirty-four years of age, a bachelor, but was very fond of boys. He had been a scoutmaster until his eyesight failed (he had had very severe cataracts). Both my brother and I had imbibed the teaching that "baptism was essential to salvation". As Mr. T. was a member of the Church of Christ, and seemed very approachable, we felt that he was the right person to speak with about this "all-important matter". Again, however, my courage failed me, and it was little Geoffrey who broached the matter. The result was that both of us were interviewed by the deacons of whom there were seven. They seemed satisfied that I "knew what I was doing". Geoffrey, however, was two years younger (he was twelve), and they felt that he should wait until he was older. At this Geoffrey burst into tears, and this moved the tender-hearted deacons to change their minds. We were both baptised on a cold winter's day in July, 1921, and made history, for I think we were the first children to be baptised by the Church of Christ in Cape Town.

Was I born again then? I find it difficult to answer this question. To be quite frank, I do not really know how far I had come spiritually by the time I joined the Church of Christ. Outwardly there was a real change. I was no longer guilty of the outlandish sins which had so disfigured my young life. I attended church with unfailing regularity, and began to take part in the services, reading the Scriptures, and praying. At the age of seventeen I was made secretary, and soon after, I began to preach.

With all this outward activity I enjoyed no fellowship with God. Prayer was like talking into empty air. The Bible was a dry book. I could get little out of it. Thus, when I began to preach I was in real difficulty. I gave a series of talks borrowed from a book I had been reading, hoping that the hearers would think that they were my own creation. I was, therefore, very embarrassed when one of the members innocently remarked, "I have read these addresses in Phillip Mauro's book." I was on a safer wicket when later on, unbeknown to any of the others, I commenced to attend a monthly meeting in Cape Town. I was able to steal the sermons I heard there, and pass them off as my own.

I had a terrible temper, and I made life almost "hell on earth" for my family. Every morning before I left for the office (I had commenced work at the age of sixteen) there was a row, always of my making. My poor mother lived in daily terror of my unreasonable fits of passion. In an effort to placate me, she let me have my own way in everything, but this only served to make me more domineering. I had become the slave of impurity, and my thought-life was a cage of unclean birds. I became increasingly concerned about all this, and tried desperately to conquer my bad habits and besetting sins. I can still see myself as I stood in the silence of my own room and clenched my fists saying, "I shall not do these things again tomorrow. I will overcome." Alas! The next evening I had to look back upon a day of dismal failure. After four years of earnest resolution, followed week after week by humiliating defeat, I was sick and tired of all my own efforts. I had learned by bitter experience that man, even religious man, is "without strength"

(Rom. 5:6) morally and spiritually. By then I was convinced, and thoroughly convinced, that sin was too strong for me.

Unfortunately, there was apparently no one in the church I attended who could shew me the better way. I do not want to be unfair, or hypercritical, but I cannot remember once hearing a message on the victorious life—holiness, prayer, humility, or any of the Christian virtues. The so-called "Bible study" seemed to be devoted almost exclusively to discussions, and sometimes heated arguments on doctrinal matters, presented in such a way that they were almost entirely divorced from daily Christian living. How good it was of the Lord, in His matchless grace, to lead me to those who could "expound to me the way of God more perfectly" (Acts 18:26).

CHAPTER 3

UNTIL HE FIND IT
(Luke 15:4)

In the midst of this mental turmoil my appendix burst, and I had to be rushed into hospital. As I lay on the operating-table, waiting for the chloroform, for the first time in my young life, I looked eternity full in the face. When I was well and death seemed far away I would have been most indignant if anyone had suggested that I was not a Christian. In that moment of reality, however, I realised that I had no assurance that I was ready to meet God.

One day an Anglican clergyman was visiting one of his parishioners. My bed was the nearest to the door of that large hospital ward and just as he was going out, this minister, the Rev. A. W. Blaxall, felt a strange urge to talk to me. I had never seen him before and he, of course, did not know who I was but in the course of the conversation Mr. Blaxall said, "I attend a monthly inter-denominational meeting in Cape Town, and have received much benefit from it. I will ask the Secretary to send you a notice each month."

For the sake of courtesy I thanked him, but had absolutely no intention of going. The teaching I had received in the "Church of Christ" still clung very closely to me, and I felt that I would be a traitor if I attended any other meetings but those of my own denomination.

When Mr. Blaxall noticed that I did not come he wrote me a letter, to which I did not reply: then a second one, but still no answer. Finally he rang my office. I still do not know how he had found out where I was working. Mr. Blaxall told me that as that day was the third Thursday of the month there would be a meeting that very evening, commencing at 5.00 p.m. I told him I was afraid that I would not be able to get there at that time, as I usually had to work late on a Thursday. This was the exact truth, but for the first time (as far as I can remember) I was off early that particular Thursday.

As, however, no specific promise had been made to Mr. Blaxall, and really not wishing to go to the meeting, I walked up from the Docks, where my office was situated, in two minds. The thought came, "If my tram comes I will catch it." As these trams followed

16

each other at short intervals it seemed certain, that at any rate that day I would not be at the meeting. When, however, the tram was not at the usual spot of boarding, I walked along the path the tram was due to come. Almost half a mile had been traversed and still no sign of the elusive tram. By that time I had reached the corner of the street in which the hall was to be found. Acting on a sudden impulse I decided to walk in.

Even now I blush when I think of the condition in which I imposed myself upon those well-dressed ladies and gentlemen. In those days I was working for Irvin and Johnson, a very large trawling and whaling firm. My job on Mondays and Thursdays was to sell fish to the big wholesale buyers, and I had a special suit to wear on those occasions, for inevitably my clothes were impregnated by the all-pervasive fish-odour.

Some time after this I went into the office of the "South Africa General Mission" to see the Superintendent about a spiritual problem. When I had gone, the two lady secretaries said to one another, "He has left his fish; I can smell it." When after searching high and low they found nothing, they realised that it was only my smell I had left in their office.

To make matters worse I propped myself in, smell and all, between two cultured ladies. They were fortunately two gracious, Christlike women. If they were shocked, they certainly did not betray it. Instead they gave me such a warm welcome that I felt thoroughly at home.

The preacher that afternoon expounded Romans 6, and then made an appeal. I must have conquered at least some of the shyness which had afflicted me in Mr. Elliot's meetings, for I stood with a few others to show that I was seeking that life where sin would "not have dominion over me" (Romans 6:14). I was not, however, dealt with, and got nowhere, but from that time onwards attended those monthly gatherings, known as "The Victorious Life Conference". These had been started some years before by the Misses Garratt, the Irish ladies who also founded the "Africa Evangelistic Band".

Fortunately I had learned wisdom in the meantime, and went home first, had a bath and changed into decent clothes. This meant that I missed the first session altogether, but had the benefit of the other two. I went with motives which were very mixed, partly to reinforce my preaching, with sermons which I could not find by myself in the Word of God. But also, I am sure, because there was a hunger in my heart for the message I heard there.

On one of these occasions I was handed a notice of the bimonthly conference of the "Junior Evangelical Fellowship of Cape Town". This had been called into being the previous year, mainly as the result of the conviction of two young Christians, a theological student and a lady teacher. These two had felt the need of a body, which would unite, in fellowship and service, young believers from all the recognised churches. I attended this conference, and was deeply impressed by the messages which the speakers, two young men both twenty-two years of age, brought.

I also learned there that a "Gospel March" was to be held the following Saturday in Woodstock (the suburb nearest to the centre of Cape Town). That Saturday afternoon I was certainly "halting between two opinions" (I Kings 18:21). On the one hand was the voice of my religious upbringing, which cried, "You cannot go. This 'Fellowship' is a hotchpotch of the very denominations you have been taught to avoid." On the other hand was the quiet, yet mighty voice, of my hungry heart.

Hardly knowing what I was doing, I found my feet, (or was it my heart?) carrying a soul, which was a whirl of conflicting emotions, in the direction of Woodstock.

Finally, I reached the "Woodstock and Salt River Railway". By then it was about 4.20 p.m., and the "Gospel March" had been timed to commence at 3.30 p.m. The hall appeared to be deserted. I said to myself, "I am hopelessly too late; they must have left. I will go somewhere else." Just at that critical moment, a lady came up to me and explained, "They are still inside, having a prayer meeting. I only came out because the baby was crying." That sentence gave my hesitating soul the push I needed, and in I went.

In a few minutes the march was under way. I found myself carrying a huge banner-text with Donald, a young man who later became a Presbyterian minister. We marched through the streets of that thickly populated suburb, singing as we went, and holding short open-airs in strategic spots. For the first time in my life I was exposed to young, robust, vital Christianity. The shining faces, the burning testimonies, the singing so full of evident joy in Christ and His salvation, awakened in my breast yearnings no language can describe.

In November of the previous year a Mr. Hugh Cartwright had visited the hospital ward in which I was lying. I had heard something about him, and wanted so much to meet him. I, therefore, pretending to read it, held my Bible well aloft, hoping he would see it. This was a change with a vengeance for, up to that point, I had only read the Scriptures (and that wasn't very often) in the semi-gloom under the sheets. You see, if one of my fellow-patients had seen me reading a Bible he might have smiled. That would have been awful, wouldn't it? What a ridiculous thing the fear of man is!

Anyhow my little plan worked. Mr. Cartwright did see my Bible, and did speak to me. Mr. Cartwright had been Head Accountant in his father's firm, one of the large departmental stores of Cape Town, but had given up his position to devote all his time to Christian work. Amongst other things he had built up a splendid library of sound Christian literature. These books he would lend out, quite free of charge, to anyone who would like to read them. Indeed, Mr. Cartwright would deliver the books to the reader, and then come and fetch them. This refined Christian gentleman was a familiar sight, walking rapidly through the streets of Cape Town, with this large case, full of books, strapped to his back.

I am glad to say that I did not allow Mr. Cartwright to do this for me, but each month I would go to his home, and borrow four or five books. He always made you feel that you were doing him a favour in using his books. He would, however, hastily add, "If you have not time for the Bible and my books, choose the Word of God and leave my books."

I mainly chose life-stories, and the reading of these great biographies increased the deep hunger of my heart. I noticed that prayer was one of the chief formative factors in the lives of these men and women of God. I decided that lack of prayer was one of the reasons why I had an unsatisfactory experience. So, every evening that I did not have a meeting or a class, I would go to a disused quarry, and kneel at a stone, which seemed as if it had been specially shaped for the purpose. I would pray there from 7.30— 9.30 p.m. Alas! I had the act, but not the spirit of prayer, and it was hard work to stay on my knees for two hours.

One night, however, as I was repeating II Corinthians 3:18 there was revealed to me, so suddenly and so unexpectedly, "the glory of the Lord". It was an experience so sacred that I have never spoken of it to anyone. I saw how unspeakably beautiful God is, and the yearning to know Him burned in my heart like a mighty fire.

One evening at "The Victorious Life Conference" there was handed to me an invitation to attend the first Annual Convention of the Africa Evangelistic Band to be held from July 19—26, 1925 at "The Towers", Muizenberg (15 miles from the centre of Cape Town), the holiday home of the Y.W.C.A.

It still seemed wrong even to want to attend meetings like that. Yet in spite of all my doubts and prejudices, I had such a longing to go—a longing I could neither explain nor understand. As I had already taken my annual leave I could not go for the whole period. We were, however, granted a free Saturday about every fourth or fifth week, and I noticed that the morning that I would be off coincided with the last week-end of the Convention. I, therefore, booked to stay at "The Towers" from the Friday evening to the Sunday night. When, however, I returned to the office I was greeted with the words, "You shouldn't have got that Saturday off." The previous week this privilege had been withdrawn, but they had omitted to tell my departmental chief. But for the forgetfulness of someone in authority, I would have never been at this Convention, for I would have thought that it was not "worthwhile" going for twenty-four hours.

It has been said that as soon as the sun hides its face, a South African becomes depressed, and that particular Friday it rained incessantly. It was thus a very gloomy South African who made his way by train to Muizenberg. My "blues" were further increased when I was met at the door by a lady. I think it dawned on me for the first time that this was a Y.W.C.A., and I felt awfully out of place. The lady said, "You have come for the Convention? I'll take you to Miss Garratt." I thought, "Oh! Women! More women!"

At that moment I just wanted to take the next train back home, but then I heard Miss Garratt say (how wise and understanding she was), "You must join the men." I was ushered into the hall in which the meetings were being held. There, sitting at the back, was a group of men, none of whom I had ever seen before. I leave you to imagine the painfully acute embarrassment of this shy little fellow. How I wished that I had never been so foolish as to let myself in for this.

Just at that moment a gentleman with a shining face and a glorious smile called out, "Come on, brother. This is the magic circle." In a second, all my strangeness melted away, and I was perfectly, exquisitely at home. I have often thought since then that, but for that sincere, hearty welcome, spoken in the power of the Spirit I might never have been blessed at that Convention, for my diffidence and prejudice might have clung round me like an elephant's hide. Now, however, I felt I "belonged", and settled down comfortably to listen.

The speaker was the Rev. Walter Searle, formerly a Congregational minister and Dr. Campbell Morgan's predecessor in Birmingham; later he became a missionary of the South Africa General Mission and a personal friend of Dr. Andrew Murray. He was now 75 years of age, but full of the fire and power of God. Of this I knew nothing. I was only conscious that God was speaking, and speaking in a very personal way.

Mr. Searle was an utter stranger to me, and yet he seemed to know all about me. He was describing my whole life with uncanny accuracy. After the benediction was pronounced, I made my way to the slopes of the mountain which rose behind "The Towers". As I knelt there for the first time in my young life, I prayed to be delivered from sin—from the evil temper and impurity, which had made my life a misery to myself and others.

As I rose from my knees I felt exactly the same as I had done before the prayer. I was so disappointed. I had so hoped something would happen. Yet I did have a joy that I had not known before, and the presence of the Lord was so real in that Convention that I revelled in the meetings. I was, however, looking for something sensational—a sudden burst of glory, an overwhelming wave of gladness. Because this had not taken place, I concluded that the Lord had not answered my prayer.

Yet, in spite of my lack of faith, the Lord was graciously working in my heart. As a result of reading the biographies I had borrowed from Mr. Cartwright I realised that, if I wanted to be really blessed, I would have to "lay all on the altar", and I sought to do so. I would hand over to the Lord one thing after another until I came to the cherished idol—my ambitions. I would indeed say, "Lord, I lay my plans, my future upon the altar", only to discover quickly that it had been a surrender "in word, but not in deed". Try as I would, I could not make a complete consecration.

Then the releasing word came on the Saturday night. We were having supper together, about eighty of us, I think, for it was just a small convention. Under normal circumstances, when such a large number are all speaking at the same time, it is difficult to hear what the one sitting alongside you is saying. Yet at that moment I heard a sentence, coming clear as a bell from quite another table. I do not know why the speaker was saying this, nor in what connection these words were uttered, but I knew they were God's message to me: "You are not willing, but are you willing to be made willing?"

Like all young men I enjoyed eating, but that evening I could scarcely wait to finish the meal. I rushed down to my room, fell on my knees, and said, "Lord, I am not willing, and I cannot make myself willing; but I am willing to be made willing." The next morning I woke to discover that all desire to be great, or to carry out my own plans, had gone.

CHAPTER 4

YOU HATH HE QUICKENED, WHO WERE DEAD
(Eph. 2:1)

THE following Monday, August 3, was a public holiday and I attended a conference of the Africa Evangelistic Band, held in the Strand, a large seaside town about thirty miles from Cape Town. After the morning session dear Wilfried Edmunds, whom I had met at "The Towers", very kindly invited me to lunch. He was later to become a very well known Baptist minister, and head of their missionary work in southern Africa.

After the meal was over, Wilfried asked me to have a word of prayer with him. When we rose from our knees, he asked me, "Brother, when did you get blessed?" I replied, "I don't know if anything has happened." "Oh!" said Wilfried, "The moment you prayed I knew that God had done a work in your heart."

I said nothing more, but I began to think: "It is true, the Lord did answer my prayer. I have not lost my temper for ten days, and I could not keep it for ten minutes. More than that, all the impurity is gone. I have no desire even, for the unclean side of sex. I am not merely delivered from the acts of sin, but from the desire for sin. I don't want to get cross. I don't want those suggestive books." Such a joy filled my soul when I realised that when I had "called on the name of the Lord" (Rom. 10:13), He had truly heard my cry, and "saved" (Rom. 10:13), not in sin, but *from* sin (Matt. 1:21).

About a fortnight after this, I went for a walk up Signal Hill, at the foot of which our lodgings were situated. I took out my Bible to read. I could not make out what had happened to me. It was just as if scales had fallen from the inner eyes of my soul, and I was "beholding wondrous things" (Psa. 119:18) "out of Thy Law". The Word of God had for so long been a closed Book to me.

On the Monday and Thursday of each week, and sometimes on a Wednesday, I had to be on duty by 5.30 a.m. I had about a three-mile walk to our offices in the Docks, for trams or buses were not running at that early hour. I put my alarm on to 2.50 a.m. After dressing, I would spend an hour in prayer. I have forgotten what I did when it was raining, but I still remember the thrill of those early quiet times. As I walked through those dark streets on my way to work, I felt that the Lord Jesus was at my side, revealing His Presence, assuring me of His love.

I wonder now why my mother, who was not a Christian (at least as far as I could judge), did not object to this seemingly unnecessary early rising for it meant her getting up at that "unearthly hour", as she always gave me something to eat before I left. I think it was because my dear mother was so grateful for the change which had come to her bad-tempered son that she was ready to accept some of the inconveniences which accompanied it.

Some time after this, my brother came and said very shyly, "Mother says you are quite a different boy since you went to those meetings." This was a very real encouragement to me, for I realised that they saw me with "the lid off"—just as I was—and not with the nice front I saw fit to put on in the company of other Christians. Best of all, I knew it was true! The Lord had done far more than I had asked or expected. I had sought Him for deliverance from the ugly things in my life. He had certainly done this.

The negative work was grand indeed, but the positive was even more glorious! He had made me over again—"a new creature in Christ Jesus" (II Cor. 5:17). "All things had indeed become new." It was not just that some things had altered for the better; everything had changed. I was living in a new world, and the thrill of it was upon me day and night. In one sense everything was the same. I was living in the same cramped quarters, walking the same streets, working in the same firm, existing on the same small income. Yet life was so exquisitely new, so delightfully fresh, so full of glad surprises. It was the Presence of the King, Who had come to live and feast with me (Rev. 3:20).

CHAPTER 5

TO PROCLAIM LIBERTY TO THE CAPTIVES
(Isa. 61:1)

FOR about nine months I walked in the glow of almost uninter-rupted fellowship with my heavenly Bridegroom (II Cor. 11:2). Then, alas! I allowed "earth-born" clouds to hide the beauty of that lovely Face (Isa. 33:17). The first was a love-affair. A friend and I had climbed Table Mountain with a sweet, pretty girl. I came down from the heights badly smitten. It all seemed so right. She was a keen Christian, active in Christian work, one who had stood out for God in her unsaved family. She had sacrificed a most eligible bachelor to follow the Lord. Most marvellous of all, she was willing to have this ugly little man. The only thing that was wrong was that it was not God's will, and that meant that every-thing was wrong.

I had, of course, prayed about the matter, but I was in too great a hurry, and "he that believeth shall not make haste" (Isa. 28:1). I did not give the Lord the time He often needs to break through our human limitations, and show us His will.

I became, however, increasingly conscious that this love-affair had brought "leanness in my soul" (Psa. 106:15), but it was my brother's faithfulness which really caused me to see "the error of my ways". He said, "Since you have been going with M— you have lost your power." I went almost immediately to the young lady, confessed that I had got out of the will of God, and sug-gested that we part. We did, but her love for me had gone deeper than I had realised, and the separation from the little man she had hoped would one day be her life-partner, left a wound which bled for many, and many a month. I think that, even years after, she still cherished the thought that I might return to her. Perhaps her disappointment led to secret bitterness and backsliding for, when I met her accidentally sixteen years later, I found that she had recently married an unsaved man. How careful we should be not to go barging into the delicate china-shop of a young girl's affections!

About this time, the Lord began to speak to me about the duty and privilege of personal evangelism. Through reading the life of

D. L. Moody, and the sermons of Dr. Torrey and Dr. Wilbur Chapman, I was filled with a yearning to be a "fisher of men" (Mark 1:17). Alas! I was firmly caught in the "snare of the fear of man" (Prov. 29:25), and for nearly five years I was a disobedient Christian. I do thank God that I never lost the assurance of salvation. Never for five minutes did I doubt that I was born again. But I lost the "joy of salvation".

I became more and more depressed, more and more introspective, absorbed in my own problems, with neither energy nor desire to be concerned about the needs of others. I seemed to be moving on the brink of a nervous breakdown, with strange fears and fancies, so that I was well on the way to landing in a mental institution. This affected my body. I developed acute stomach pains. My doctor thought that I had ulcers, and sent me to a specialist, but X-rays revealed nothing organically wrong. When the aches spread all over my body—sometimes I couldn't turn my neck; then again, I could scarcely walk because of the pain in my back; then it would shift to my ankle—I realised that they were all the result of my nervous condition. Oh! those were dark days indeed. The nights were scarcely better, for my sleep was haunted by persistent nightmares.

Then in the middle of 1929, a Dr. Allan came to Cape Town, and preached at "The Victorious Life Conference" on Revelation 12:11. As I walked home the Lord spoke to me through Isaiah 61:1. I could almost hear an audible voice as the Master, so tenderly said to me, "Bertram, I have come to proclaim to your captive soul, liberty."

As He spoke, the fetters of the years fell away. I awoke the next morning an utterly new person. I was gloriously well—physically and mentally, and spiritually. I felt as refreshed in mind and body as if I had had a year's holiday. But that blessing had to be maintained by faith.

The previous evening, the Lord had poured in "the oil of joy" to my wounded spirit and that afternoon by an act of the will, I put on "the garment of praise" (Isa. 61:3). I had gone out to a suburb of Cape Town on business. Instead of taking the bus or the train back, I walked four of five miles through those leafy streets, praising the Lord that He had delivered me from "the spirit of heaviness" and the burden of depression. I felt that I could not keep this wondrous joy to myself.

I remembered that every Friday night "The City Mission" held an open-air. I had never attended it before, but I had to let the gladness out. The kind friends let me speak, and I just poured out the "good tidings" of Isa. 61. This deliverance was permanent. I never returned to the bondage of those agonising years. My nervous condition was greatly improved, though not completely cured, but I was "set free to serve" (Luke 1 : 74, 75), and took part regularly in open-air meetings.

Yet with all this, I was still not able to speak to people personally about the Lord Jesus, but the Master again spoke to me at "The Victorious Life Conference". This time it was through the well-known Keswick speaker, Mr. Montagu Goodman. He brought a powerful message on the words: "I have opened my mouth unto the Lord, and I cannot go back" (Judges 11 : 35). For five years, the Lord had had a controversy with me about personal evangelism, but that night I "crossed the Rubicon", never to return again. I was always too shy to present myself to these big preachers but that night I waited until the whole hall had emptied. I just managed to blurt out, "Mr. Goodman, God has spoken to me tonight, and I am going to obey at all costs."

I realised that I had to act, and act immediately. I remembered that along the Esplanade where the City met the ocean, there was always to be found on a summer evening a row of men, nearly half-a-mile long, leaning against the railings. The next evening, a Friday, I made my way down there, a bundle of tracts in my hand. I started at the bottom of the line but by the time I reached its end, I still hadn't spoken one word, nor given out one tract.

I turned round and made my way slowly back. I can still see those standing figures, as if it were but yesterday. Those men looked so big and terrifying; I felt so small and weak. Once again I found myself at the bottom but, as for the second time I turned around, I said to myself: "I will be doing this all night. I must make a start." I just realised that I could not go back without witnessing; back to the old life of disobedience; back, perhaps, to depression and darkness.

In the middle of the row I saw a man who did not, somehow, seem as frightening as the rest. I saw the tracts and my hand go out, and I heard a voice say, "Would you like one of these?" To my amazement this gentleman said, "Oh! thank you very much." I thought, "This doesn't sound too bad."

Once again I heard that voice, which I presumed must be mine, "Excuse me. Are you interested in religion, Sir?" The ice was, at last, broken and I think I must have spoken about thirty minutes to this affable stranger about the claims of Christ. Praise the Lord for giving me the grace not only to begin, but also to persevere.

I have sought to witness to, at least, one soul a day (as Moody did), and in the intervening years I have spoken of Jesus and His love in many lands, in all kinds of places, in three languages and in every conceivable form of transport (except a submarine). One a day seems very little, but in the passage of years it has amounted to tens of thousands. To Him, Who has so graciously broken the galling fetters of craven fear, be all the glory. Yet I must not leave a wrong impression. This God-given courage has not meant a deliverance from fear, but rather the ability to do the right in spite of fear (1 Cor. 2:3). The Lord has not made witnessing easy, but possible.

CHAPTER 6

FILLED WITH THE SPIRIT OF GOD TO WORK
(Exodus 31:3, 4)

I ONCE read of an employer who was interviewing an applicant for work in his firm. "Why did you leave your previous job?" he asked. "My boss said he was losing money with what I was making." "What were you making?" "Mistakes, Sir."

I had lost two positions, with excellent prospects in large and important firms, because of inefficiency, and found myself unemployed at the worst possible time. It was the beginning of the world-wide depression of the 1930's. One would answer an advertisement only to find that there were scores, if not hundreds, applying for the same vacancy. I did not feel I could use the references I had because they did not really speak the truth. My previous employers, in order to help me, had given a wrong impression as to my abilities. My appearance was against me. The interviewer was, no doubt, saying to himself: "This fellow certainly does not look up to much." Finally I took on a job as steward on a ship. I was provided with quarters, food, and a uniform, so that my need was met. The salary was, however, pitifully small, so that I was able to give very little help to my mother.

Finally, a gentleman, who scarcely knew me (I had only met him once before), offered me employment. I had to start at the bottom, as I had not been in that line of business. There were, however, prospects of advancement and I gratefully accepted the position. The tests soon came.

One afternoon the manager of this Builders' Hardware Company came to me and said, "Mr. X. has called us on the phone. His clients are coming to look at baths, basins, locks, etc., which are to be installed in the house he is building for them. You must add 10% to all the prices. Mr. X. has assured us that we are quite safe. He has told these people that we are an honest firm, and that they don't need to go anywhere else." I replied, "Mr. G. I cannot do this. Every time I give a false price I will be telling a lie. I will be helping this builder to defraud his clients, and will be taking a mean advantage of their trust in our honesty."

The manager was very angry, I suppose because my attitude

condemned him, for he was a regular church-goer and would, I think, have liked to be regarded as a Christian. He was a very good-living and high-principled man, and this kind of underhand business "went against the grain". Indeed he said, "I don't like this any more than you, but what are we to do? All the other hardware firms go in for this kind of thing and, if we refuse, we will lose all our clients and go bankrupt."

The other clerks were not angry. They looked at me with amusement and yet with pity. They wondered what kind of strange creature the wind had blown in. They said, "Man, if you are not willing to tell lies you will never get on in business." I really expected to get the order of the boot, for I knew that the manager, just with a snap of the fingers, could have got dozens of other young fellows who would have jumped at the chance of a job. For years the manager had his knife into my brother, who had joined the firm some months after I had, and me. With the rest of the staff we were under a cloud. BUT the Lord, "by that working whereby He is able even to subdue all things unto Himself" (Phil. 3 : 21), kept us in the firm.

After I had been working for this Builders' Hardware Company for five and a half years, the managership of our branch store became vacant. "Mac", a South African born Scot, had joined our staff, and it was decided to put him in charge, with myself as his assistant. He, however, knew practically nothing about hardware, and I realised that I would have to run the store, while "Mac" took the credit for managing the business, and the salary which went with it. After much earnest thought and prayer, I went to see Mr. Williamson, the leader of our open-air band, "a man full of wisdom and the Holy Ghost." He advised, "Bertram, have a frank talk with Mr. G. Don't demand the managership, but say that you feel you are entitled to be considered for that position in view of the length of your service for the firm."

I did just this. Mr. G. was anything but encouraging. "Bertram, if you fail now, you will fail for ever. If you make a hash of this job you can never be considered again for promotion." I realised afterwards that, what Mr. G. meant was, "You are still young. Wait until you become more experienced and efficient."

At the time, however, it sounded to me (probably because I was over-sensitive) as if he thought: "Well, of course, you will fail; we cannot expect anything better of you." This was crushing, especially to a person of my temperament. I was, therefore, surprised to hear myself replying, "I feel I ought to be given the opportunity of showing whether I am capable of holding down this job or not." Mr. G. had another fear: "I don't think you could control the men under you. You could not lose your temper with them." I replied, "I could make them obey me." Finally Mr. G. said, "I don't think you have any chance, but I will go and see Mr. O." Mr. G. came back and said: "Mr. O. (he was the owner of the firm) "says that we must give you a chance."

It was decided that I should commence in about three weeks time, long enough to give me a bad attack of the jitters. The Monday I was due to begin was "April Fools' Day" (April 1st). I wondered if I was not a prize fool in applying for a job which was too big for me? Was Mr. G. not right in suggesting that I would not be able to control the staff? What about E.? He has a strong personality; will he bow to my authority? What about J., old enough to be my father? And there is "Mac", full of chagrin because he has lost the job he was certain he was going to get. Will he not watch me as a cat watches a mouse—the slightest mistake magnified, and duly reported to Mr. O., into whose confidence he seems to have wormed his way? Have I really got "what it takes" to run a business?

I awoke that Monday morning early enough to have a long, unhurried season of waiting on God. I prayed just for one thing—my new job. By the time I had to leave for work, I knew that God had answered me in my "day of trouble" (Psalm 50:15). There was still nervous tension, yet beneath all those fears there was a quiet assurance that the Lord was going to be to me all I needed.

And He was! He enabled me to do my work so efficiently that neither Mr. G. nor Mr. O. would hear of my being transferred back to the main store, as had been the practice in the past. This was to keep the managers of the branch store in touch with the "indoor hardware", which was only stocked in the main shop. My superiors, however, seemed to think that the advantage they would gain by my being fully conversant with both sides of the business was outweighed by the fact that I had been able to eliminate the mistakes which had been losing them customers.

I believe that the Lord gave me the same anointing which He had bestowed on Bezaleel (Exodus 31:1-5). He could say of me, as He did of that labourer of old, "I have filled him with the Spirit of God, in wisdom, and in understanding, and in knowledge, and in all manner of workmanship." When I finally left to go into evangelistic work, the same Mr. G. said such flattering things about my managerial ability that I was glad that he had chosen to do so over the phone, so that he could not see my painful blushes.

The Lord also graciously undertook in the difficult sphere of "public relations" so that I had "favour with all the people" (Acts 2:47). The customers seemed to like and trust me, and I believe that I was able to attract quite a lot of new business to the company, and to do this without any questionable methods. Sometimes a man would come in and buy an article. For instance a tap: he would ask, "How much does it cost?" I would reply, "Five shillings." The customer would then say, "Please make out the receipt for eight shillings. I am working for a very difficult man. He is trying to beat me down for every penny, and I must make a little somehow." I would invariably reply, "I am sorry, but we don't do that kind of thing here."

I would say to myself, "That is the last time I will see that man." But so often he would be back the next day! I suppose he thought, "If this fellow will not help me to do my client, he will not do me either." Indeed, if Mr. G. could not convince a customer he would call me on the phone and say, "Mr. X. is listening in. He does not seem to believe me. Would you tell him what the position is?" I would explain matters and would then hear Mr. G. say, "You hear what Friend says; are you satisfied?" Mr. X. would reply, "Yes, thank you. If Friend says so I know it is true."

The Lord also gave me, in quite a remarkable way, the confidence and the affection of the staff so that they often went out of their way to help me. "Mac" seemed to quite get over his disappointment and we worked very happily together. Later on he was promoted to be secretary of the company. Best of all, the Lord gave me "the light of His countenance" so that I was wonderfully conscious of His presence amid all the humdrum of the workaday world.

After I had gone into evangelistic work, my brother was promoted to be manager of the same store. Sometimes I visited him there and felt a strange tug at my heart when I thought of the days there, amid the pipes and the nails, the rats and the cobwebs. "I had walked with One, that One the Son of God."

CHAPTER 7

DO THE WORK OF AN EVANGELIST
(II Tim. 4 : 5)

It was August Bank Holiday, 1939. I was sitting on the platform of the conference hall in the grounds of the Africa Evangelistic Band Bible College. I had been one of the speakers at that holiday gathering. The chairman of the meeting, the late Mr. L. Sheasby, then the A.E.B. Superintendent for the whole of the Cape Province, turned to me, "Would you be able to come to Worcester to take part in our convention which commences there on December 9?" Why he asked me I really do not know, for when I arrived there I found that he had quite a galaxy of preachers—two Pilgrims of the A.E.B., a most godly minister, a greatly used evangelist and a convention speaker of international repute. But I believe the Lord led Mr. Sheasby to give this invitation in order to give me the final prod I needed to come to a decision.

Ever since I had been born again, I had longed to go into "whole-time service". It was, however, from October, 1936 that this yearning became like "fire shut up within my bones". Almost daily I prayed about this voice within. Was it really the call of God? (Isa. 6 : 8). I was so afraid to make a mistake. I had a mother dependent on me and a lassie who was one day to be my wife. What would happen to them if I left the safety of an assured salary for "the hand-to-mouth existence" of an itinerant evangelist?

I promised to give Mr. Sheasby a speedy answer and, on Friday, August 11, 1939 I knelt at my bedside after supper, determined to stay there until I was certain of the Lord's leading. After some hours in prayer I felt free to write and tell Mr. Sheasby that I would come to Worcester. When, a couple of years later, I read the life of Charles Cowman, I was interested to see that that great soul received his call to missionary service in the East on August 11, when he too, like I, was 32 years of age.

I must, however, hasten to confess that I did not have the same clear call to which other workers for God can testify. This has led to a great deal of uncertainty throughout my life. Often, when things have apparently gone wrong, or my ministry has seemed fruitless, I have been sorely tempted to feel that I had made a mistake. Yet perhaps you may feel, as I have come to believe, that the Lord, by opening doors of opportunity, by providing all our temporal needs and, above all, by giving "fruit which does remain" (John 15:16), has graciously demonstrated that the decision of August 11 was "ordained of God".

I had, however, scarcely made this decision when Hitler invaded Poland and all the horrors of a world-conflict burst upon our Western civilisation. South Africa decided to enter the war. Mr. Williamson, our open-air and prayer-meeting leader and a great man of God, came to me with all the authority of an old soldier (as a young man he had been a member of the famous Scottish regiment, "The Black Watch"). "Bertram," he said, "this war is going to be much worse than the previous one, and I think you will find it almost impossible to do evangelistic work. I doubt very much indeed if the Africa Evangelistic Band" (he was a Council member of the A.E.B.) "will be able to continue holding services." This, coming from such a source, troubled me quite a lot.

Then the Lord graciously spoke to me from Daniel 11. I felt this chapter described conditions very much like those in which we now found ourselves and that, therefore, the thirty-second verse had a special message for that very time: "BUT the people that do know their God shall be strong and DO." You will have noticed that the word 'exploits' is in italics, showing that it is not in the original text. It came home to me that the Lord was calling His Church, not to restrict her activities because of the war, but rather to advance to new and daring ventures of faith. It was clear that the Master wanted us to be 'doers', not retreaters.

There were, however, other and more personal obstacles. One was my physical condition. My faithful, candid friend, George, said to me, "How can you think of full-time service? You have scarcely enough energy for your daily work." This was perfectly true. At times I could scarcely walk, because of the acute nervous pains from which I suffered.

Mr. Williamson felt that the state of my health would make it impossible for me to be accepted as a worker in the Africa Evangelistic Band. I had never trusted the Lord for my body, and indeed was irritated when anyone spoke of the possibility of "Divine Healing". Every year we seemed to have a mild "flu" epidemic in Cape Town, and in September, 1939 I realised that I had, once again, picked up the germ. I was feeling so "rotten" that I had only one desire—to get into bed and stay there for a few days.

When, however, I arrived home, I found Mr. Williamson in

bed (I boarded with him), and heard that, at least, two other members of our band were down with the "flu". I thought to myself, "If we all get sick, what is going to happen to the prayer-meeting and to the open-air?" I walked into my bedroom, got on my knees, and said, "Lord, would You please heal me tonight and grant that I may arise in the morning perfectly well?"

The Lord literally answered that prayer. The next day there was not a trace of the "flu", and I was feeling "on top of the world". That little prayer launched me out on a life-long experience of taking "the Lord for the body" (I Cor. 6:13) and today, at the age of 68, I enjoy splendid health. It is years since I last had to spend a day in bed.

Even after this, however, it seemed as if my path to a life of effective evangelism was hedged up with thorns. Indeed, I avoided mentioning that I was planning to go into "whole-time service", for I noticed that the reaction on the part of my fellow-believers was nearly always one of embarrassment. They wanted to wish me well, and yet felt that they could not do so sincerely, so certain were they that I was making a terrible mistake.

For this I think there were three main reasons. First: the state of my health. Second: the fact that I had a mother dependent on my being able to earn. Third, and most of all: because I was going out as a free-lance evangelist.

I loved the A.E.B., and would very much have liked to enter their ranks. The allowance, however, though more than enough to meet the need of an individual worker, was not sufficient to support my mother. They must, however, have wondered how I could ever have thought that anyone would ever ask a little un-known man, like me, to conduct special services. My preaching experience had been almost entirely limited to street-meetings, and open-air speakers, at any rate in Cape Town, were rather despised. The only encouragement came from my dear brother, Geoffrey. He said to me, "No, I believe you are doing the right thing. The trouble is we do not venture out enough upon God." I realised that these were not empty words, for if I was not able to give my share of my mother's support, it would come down very heavily upon my brother, and he was already married, while I was still single.

I had joined the firm in September and my annual leave was, therefore, due in that month. After I had been there, however, for two or three years, my boss asked me to take it in December. I explained, "But, sir, it is not due for another nine months." He replied, "That does not matter. December suits us better, for that is the month when all the builders take their holiday."

The temptation came to me: By now they have quite forgotten that you are only entitled to your leave in September. Don't say anything about it, and you will get a fortnight's pay in lieu of your annual holiday.

I decided, however, to be perfectly honest. I went to Mr. G. and explained matters. He listened and then said, "You are leaving on December 9. If, therefore, we pay you a third of a month's salary, you will be satisfied?" I could not truthfully say that I would be "satisfied", for, right inside, I had cherished the hope that I would get a bit more. I, therefore, merely said, "That is all I'm entitled to."

Just before I left, however, Mr. G. came to me and said, "I have received a letter from the Boss." (This was from Mr. O. who was on holiday in England). "He says we must give you a full month's pay and, because you are going out in this type of work, another £25."

I spent December taking part in the Worcester Convention, and in helping with beach services. The first part of January, I attended the annual convention of the Africa Evangelistic Band, held in Cape Town. While there Mr. Von Staden asked me to come to Vereeniging, in the Transvaal, to be an Afrikaans Speaker at the convention to be held in the Methodist Church there. I must say of this invitation, as I could of the one to Worcester, "This was the Lord's doing, and is marvellous in our eyes." My presence there seemed utterly unnecessary. Not only was Mr. Cuthbertson, a much-used convention speaker of international repute, there, but Mr. Von Staden had the help of his wife, who was a very fine preacher indeed and three Afrikaans-speaking Pilgrims of outstanding ability. "But God"! He wanted me in the Transvaal, as subsequent events were to show so clearly.

The Vereeniging Convention was only to commence more than a month later. I had, however, nothing to do in the Cape and decided to go on immediately to the Transvaal, trusting the Lord to open a door of ministry which would keep me occupied during the intervening weeks. Mr. Von Staden asked me to take one of the Pilgrims with me and, on Thursday morning, January 17, 1940, I left on the first leg of my gipsy wanderings for Jesus—a 1,000 mile trip in my Studebaker Commander (14 miles to the gallon, if I was fortunate!) to Johannesburg. I soon ran into trouble. First of all my fan-belt broke and I had to drive twenty miles with a red-hot engine in the blistering heat of mid-summer until I was able to buy a new belt in the next town.

But that was only the beginning! Three tyres burst, and I had to buy four new ones. The last horror was an awful grinding noise, as if every bit of the engine was being chewed up. It was a relief to discover that it was only the speedometer-cable, which had broken. And how good of the Lord to put it into the heart of my boss to give me the exact amount of money which He saw I would need to cover all the costs of that nightmare trip!

It did, however, mean that practically all my money was gone. I can still feel my thumping heart as I drove into Johannesburg at about 10.00 a.m. on Saturday, January 19, with only 10/- in my pocket, and £1 in my Post Office Savings Account. I knew no one in all that great city, except one fellow-believer whom I had only met at A.E.B. conferences. I had nowhere to go, and certainly no money to pay for hotel accommodation. Yet within twenty-four hours I had already commenced a fortnight's series of special meetings. Dear believers who had never looked me in the face before and who knew nothing of my preaching ability, except that they had heard that I had "been on A.E.B. platforms", had dared to do the unusual and had invited "this little unknown" to conduct an evangelistic campaign in their church.

In the more than thirty-four years which have passed since that day, the Lord has graciously kept me busy in the work of His Kingdom, and is still giving me opportunities for service. I was able to support my mother until her death; to get married at the Lord's time, and to bring up a family. He also "gave me the desire of my heart" (Psalm 37:4), and made it possible for me to become an A.E.B. worker.

After the Vereeniging Convention I was conducting a fortnight's mission with another A.E.B. Pilgrim when a most gracious letter from my brother, Geoffrey, arrived. He said that he had received a considerable rise in salary and that he would now be able to give a larger amount to our mother. The figure I had to contribute to her support, was now exactly the sum I would receive as a Pilgrim. I wondered if this was not a sign that the Master was leading me into the A.E.B.

While I was still pondering this, I went to take part in an Easter camp convention, held by the A.E.B. I had to speak nine times in my very broken Afrikaans but the Lord worked with unusual power, revealing His glory through a very earthen vessel (II Cor. 4:7). At the close, Mr. Von Staden came to me, "Would you not consider becoming a Pilgrim?" I replied, "That seems to be the way the Lord is leading me." He wrote immediately. Miss Helena Garratt, Founder and Secretary of the Africa Evangelistic Band, wired back, "Accept Friend straight away." After more than thirty-four years I am still in the A.E.B., and still count it a great privilege to serve the Master in their ranks.

CHAPTER 8

WHOSO FINDETH A WIFE FINDETH A GOOD THING
(Prov. 18:22)

AFTER the tragic mistake I made with dear M. I decided to give myself seven months to pray through about any future love-affair before I gave any indication, either to the lady in question or to anyone else, that my heart was leaping in a certain direction. For eleven years this decision, inspired, I believe, by the Holy Spirit, kept me from a second mistake. I blush to think of the many times I had an agitation within, "an ache where you cannot scratch it" (as my wife expressed it), but before the seven months were up the affection had worn off.

The single exception was W., a gentle, sweet girl, who captured more than one heart. My tender feelings towards her persisted for two or three years until in desperation I took my brother into my confidence. My dream-castles came crashing to the ground when Geoffrey said, "She and L. are practically engaged." This was a shock indeed. Yet how grateful I was that this decision, not to make advances until I was certain that an affection was the will of God, had saved W. and me, both of us very shy people, from sore embarrassment.

Thus, by the time I had reached the age of thirty I was regarded as a confirmed bachelor, that is, until a Saturday evening in September, 1937. The previous week Geoffrey had come to me and said, "Bertram, we are not playing the game with the girls. We treat them as if they do not exist. All of us young fellows go off after every open-air and prayer-meeting without ever a word to them. We ought to think a bit more about the social side of our lives."

I felt this was reasonable and determined that the next Saturday evening I would remain behind for a few minutes and try and exchange a few words with the girls. The other young men must have been thinking as I was, for I found that everyone of our young ladies was in conversation: everyone, that is with the exception of "Babsie" Fourie. As no one else was available I decided to do my duty and talk to her. She was only a year old spiritually, but I was deeply impressed by her love for the Master and her joy in His salvation. I don't think we spoke for more than five minutes but the deed was done! Cupid's arrow had pierced my bachelor-heart and penetrated very deeply.

I worked on Saturdays only until 1.00 p.m. The remainder of the afternoon was devoted to my mother and I managed to "kill two birds with one stone". I would call for my mother at her home, take her to some beauty spot where she would sit quite contentedly in the car, reading the "Weekend Argus", while I went off for a walking quiet-time.

Cape Town, with its lovely mountain-paths, was an ideal spot for this combined spiritual and physical exercise. I believe my dear heavenly Master, so considerate and so wise, led me to this form of waiting on Him. My body needed the fresh-air and exercise, but, if it had been a purely physical thing, I would have grudged taking the time from prayer.

What, however, I really wanted to say was that the following Saturday I dared to ask Babsie and another girl to accompany my mother and me on a drive. They accepted my invitation but I shudder to think of how I treated them. When we reached Constantia Nek, with its sylvan scenes and glorious view, I left my mother in the car and my two lady passengers sitting on a rock, while I went off praying for nearly two hours. I think Babsie and Hester spent the time pleasantly and profitably praying and meditating, but they must have thought it a strange way to give two young girls a Saturday afternoon outing.

The next time we were together, I had taken Babsie for a run on a weekday afternoon at about 5.30 p.m., when I had finished work. I discovered that Babsie was very keen to improve her driving ability. She had had some experience with her brothers' vehicles, but did not yet have a licence. So I said to myself, "Here's the way. 'Say it with cars, and not with flowers.' "

On this trip, therefore, when we reached a fairly quiet road, I handed the wheel to Babsie. She made some demur, and yet I could see that she was pleased. I never felt nervous with her even in heavy traffic, for her reactions were quick, and she never did anything stupid. This, however, commenced a tug-of-war in my little heart. If I took Babsie out I felt guilty, for I did not yet have the assurance that this love was the will of God. Yet, if to satisfy my conscience, I stayed away, the hunger to be with her and the yearning to do things for her, almost overwhelmed me.

Babsie had been teaching a Sunday School class in the "City Mission", situated in "District Six", at that time a notorious slum area. On December 1, 1937, she decided to visit her scholars and their parents. When I heard of this, (I think if I remember rightly, from one of her fellow Sunday School teachers), the battle began again. How I longed to help her. Yet could I? Dare I? Was I not playing with fire, as I had done with dear M. years before? Was I not awakening in my own soul and in the heart of this young believer, the flame of a carnal passion?

As these conflicting thoughts were raging within I heard a quiet Voice, speaking in the silences of my soul, "Go and fetch Babsie. You will be glad, later on, that you have done so." As soon as I had finished work, I hurried up to the City Mission in my car and found that I had not been mistaken. In a few minutes she arrived there. As we had some time to spare before she needed to be back at the Y.W.C.A., where she was lodging, I suggested that we drive up Signal Hill, from which vantage point one had magnificent views of the City and of the Bay. As we were praying together in the car, I heard again the Voice of the Shepherd (John 10:4), "She is the wife I have chosen for you."

The next Wednesday, with a very big lump in my throat, I took Babsie down to the station. She was taking her teacher's course at the Technical College, and was now en route to the Transvaal, where she was to spend the long summer holiday at her parents' home in Christiana, a country town about seventy miles to the north of Kimberley, the "Diamond City".

It was awful to think of this separation, lasting nearly two months. I managed, however, to scrape all my courage together and asked, "Could I write to you?" Babsie gave her consent very readily. I then told her that I was keen to improve my Afrikaans, which was very poor indeed, as I had not learnt it at school (I had taken French and Latin instead). I was thrilled with her answer: "If you want to learn Afrikaans you will be very welcome in my home" (Babsie's parents were both Afrikaans speaking).

I decided to accept this wonderful invitation, and to spend my annual holiday which was due in a few weeks' time, at Christiana. My train pulled into that country station at about 11.15 p.m. What a sight it was for a love-hungry heart to see my sweetheart darting out of the darkness with leaping steps to meet "the little man from Cape Town". It seemed that I did not need clearer proof that she cared for me in a special way. It was therefore, with great confidence that the following evening I declared my love for her. The sentence at the end, "Do you think you could love me in return?" would be met, I was convinced, by a very decided and glad "Yes". You can, therefore, imagine my dismay when Babsie replied, "Well, now, that is a very difficult question to answer."

The next day Babsie explained more fully that boys had been

one of the great idols in her unconverted life. She had laid her affections completely on the altar, and had now no other desire but to give the whole of her life to the Master Who had so utterly conquered her heart. What I did not know then, but was to learn later, was that, even if Babsie had considered marriage, I would not be in the picture at all. She confided in a girl-friend (who was kind enough to tell me the truth, so that I would not live in a fools' Paradise): "I could never think of marrying Bertram; he would get on my nerves. He is a bundle of nerves. My place in the prayer-meeting is just behind him, and he never sits still, even for a minute." I did not realise then that I had already become a rather eccentric bachelor, with a host of habits which few girls could stand.

Babsie was very considerate and wise. She did not creep into her shell after this unwelcome proposal, but treated me most graciously as a welcome guest and a valued brother in Christ. We had long and interesting talks about the things of God, but ONE subject was taboo. Once, indeed, I did very gingerly suggest that perhaps we would one day become lover and sweetheart, but Babsie kindly, but most firmly said, "You must please never mention that matter again."

Despite the graciousness of Babsie and the kindness of her parents, the holiday, to which I had looked forward so eagerly, became a nightmare. My darling was so near and yet so far. I can still feel the darkness of those days at Christiana when my sun seemed to go down at noonday and all my hopes had perished.

I returned to Cape Town to meet a very critical brother. He told me that my mother had been almost beside herself with distress at the thought of my cherishing affection for "an Afrikaans girl". Although she had grown up in a Dutch-speaking country town, my mother was very English in her outlook and very prejudiced against the "Boers". She was determined that I should have nothing to do with them or their language and it was for that reason that I had not learned Afrikaans at school.

Geoffrey did not share her feelings but he did say to me, "We cannot think of marriage; we have a mother to support." I replied, "Geoffrey, I am thirty and you nearly twenty-nine. If we are not to get married at our age, when will we ever be able to do so?" Perhaps this was the encouragement Geoffrey needed, for within a month of this conversation, he was privately engaged to the girl who was to become his wife, and they have already had more than thirty-five years of very happy married life, with two lovely children.

Unfortunately, I did not tell Geoffrey or anyone else that there was really nothing between Babsie and me. I thought, "The other Christians think a lot of me. They feel that I know the mind of the Lord and do the will of God but if I confess that I have made such a terrible mistake, I will lose all my influence with them." I let them keep the impression, which my visit to Christiana had created, that Babsie and I were meant for each other. This was not only "making a lie" (Rev. 21:27), but was a great mistake and created most embarrassing situations both for Babsie and for me. When I met her at the station it was a joy-pain situation. It was great to see her face again, and yet there was a terrible barrier between us. Babsie was obviously very ill-at-ease in my presence, and the fact that everyone regarded us as lovers made the position still worse.

On February 11, 1938, as I sat down to supper, the servant handed me a letter, addressed to me in Babsie's handwriting. Before I opened it I felt, "This is bad news." So it was. Babsie had written, "Since your visit to Christiana, I have searched my heart thoroughly. I DO NOT LOVE YOU."

I finished the meal quickly, and hurried out for a long, walking quiet-time on the slopes of Signal Hill. I wanted to say, "Lord I have greatly sinned in cherishing a romance which never should have begun." But it almost seemed as if a Divine Hand was laid upon my lips. Somehow I couldn't get the words of confession out. I could not understand it. I ought to be under deep conviction of sin, and yet I was not.

As I was making no headway with the prayer, which I was certain I should pray, I went back home and burst into Mr. Williamson's room (I was boarding with him), "Mr. Williamson, why did you say that evening last November as Babsie climbed out of my car to go into the Y.W.C.A., 'If I were a young fellow again this is the girl I would marry'?"

Mr. Williamson was very frank, "Because I could see you were in love with her," he said. This was, I think, before anyone else was aware of the fact, but this man had a wonderful gift of discernment. I replied, "Mr. Williamson, I am, but Babsie isn't. Look at the letter I have received."

To my amazement he did not, as I had done, regard this letter as the death-knell of all my hopes. "Bertram," he advised, "don't give up hope. I believe the Lord will yet give you the desire of your heart. Keep praying. Keep believing. My wife also turned me down at first, but the Lord gave me the assurance that I would win her love in the end, and I did, of course."

I was so bucked by this tonic that I actually had the cheek to invite Babsie for another drive, with Dalene as a companion. If I remember rightly Babsie went out twice with me. The third Saturday afternoon, however, I found only Dalene at the door of the Y.W.C.A. She was very frank and explained: "Babsie made some excuse, which I soon realised was not the real reason, so I was very blunt with her: 'Babsie, why do you not want to go out with Bertram?' Babsie replied, 'I don't feel it is fair to encourage him in this way when I have not the slightest intention of marrying him!'"

I made no comment, but in my heart I said, "This is final. If that is how Babsie feels, she will never be bothered by me again. Apart from brief greetings at meetings, for courtesy's sake, I will leave her severely alone."

The next evening was the Sunday night open-air. As usual, after the meeting proper we had remained behind to hand out tracts and talk to interested persons. When I had finished with my seeker, I found that all the workers had left, with the single exception of Babsie, who was still busy with a soul.

My inner being was again the battle-ground of conflicting emotions. I did not like the idea of Babsie's walking back alone through the dark streets. My heart longed to escort her home, yet . . . . I was determined not to force myself on her, not after what I had heard.

For some reason, which I have forgotten, I did not have the car that night, and I walked off. I could not, however, resist the temptation to turn back to peep round the corner just to see if she were safe. I was in process of doing this when I met Willie. "Bertram", he said, "you must go back to the open-air. Babsie wants to see you, wants to see you specially."

I was still so hurt at the thought that Babsie regarded outings with me in no better light than a painful duty, a kind of soothing syrup to be administered to a rejected lover, that I was half inclined to say: "I don't want to see her." I realised, however, that that would be neither Christlike nor courteous. So back to the open-air spot and to Babsie.

The whole walk up to the Y.W.C.A., about twelve minutes in duration, was an agony of silent embarrassment. I felt that Babsie had something on her mind, but I was determined not to prod her. Finally, as we stood at the entrance to the Y.W.C.A., Babsie managed to blurt out a single sentence, "You know what you said to me at Christiana: the Lord has shown me that you were right." I wanted to ask, "What do you actually mean?" But she had already darted from me and was fleeing up the stairs.

The next few days were passed in an agony of uncertainty. We met at the Wednesday evening prayer-meeting held each week in Mr. Williamson's home. I escorted her to the "Y", but Babsie seemed stiff and distant. I was still not sure how far I had got with her. I decided, therefore, to "take the bull by the horns" and called her on the phone the next afternoon. "Babsie, are you free? My brother is using the car, but could we go for a long walk?"

She confessed afterwards that she would have liked to decline but could think of no legitimate excuse. We had dinner together in a cafe, and went for a walk of several miles. Babsie then told me the whole story. On the Saturday afternoon, March 5, she had felt badly about having refused to go out with me. As she always did, she went with her problem to the Throne of Grace. She prayed, "Lord, I know I have hurt Bertram, and hurt him deeply, but is it right to go out with a man for whom I have no real affection?" To her surprise, the Lord asked her the same question: "Why do you not want to go out with Bertram?"

As she knelt in the quiet of "Concordia", the Prayer-Room of the Y.W.C.A., the Lord showed her the hidden motives of her heart—thoughts and desires, which had led to her rejection of my love; a fear that she would be called upon to bear many children; a shrinking from a life of poverty, which might be hers, if I was called into whole-time service; wounded pride in having a husband, who was very nervy, weedy-looking, and rather eccentric, etc., etc. The Lord had also said, "Babsie, if you want to have My best, you must be prepared to marry Bertram."

At last, at about 6.00 p.m. on Saturday, March 5th, just before the supper bell was about to ring, she finally said "Yes" to the Master's call.

The next morning Babsie had a talk with a Mrs. Ferree, a godly American missionary. She asked, "But, Babsie, are you in love with the man?" Characteristically Babsie answered, "I am not worried about that. God can give me love in a moment of time. What concerns me is: Is it the will of God?"

Yet, after having told me all this, Babsie concluded by saying, "We must just be friends." I suppose by that she meant that there should be no demonstrations of affection. I felt like replying, "This is a most unreasonable request. Indeed, I wonder if you are not asking something impossible."

Fortunately, however, I said nothing. The Master Himself worked in His own gracious way. On March 25, I called her on the phone, "Babsie, I have to go out this evening on a business trip, would you like to come with me?"

To my amazement and delight she replied, "Yes, certainly. I am longing to be with you." As we drove together that evening she said, "We must pray much that the Lord will guard our love. To me it is simply wonderful that I should love you so deeply."

More than thirty-six years have fled by since that evening in 1938, and we are still sweethearts. The God Who "setteth the solitary in families" (Psalm 68:6) kept our love warm and fresh during the more than four years, which were to elapse before we were finally married on a never-to-be-forgotten Saturday in July, 1942. For most of that four years we saw very little of each other, for my fiancée was teaching in Oudtshoorn, while I was working as a Pilgrim hundreds of miles away in the Transvaal.

CHAPTER 9

CRUCIFIED WITH CHRIST
(Gal. 2:20)

I WAS in my room. Mr. Williamson was speaking in the courtyard just outside: "George, I want you to lead the prayer-meetings and the open-airs while I am away at the Convention." I thought: "Why cannot I have a share in the leading? When Mr. Williamson was visiting Scotland two years ago he appointed George and me to be deputy-leaders in his absence. Since his return, however, for some unknown reason he never asks me to take charge of any meeting." In 1933 before he had left for Scotland Mr. Williamson had stood in the crowd, while George had led the open-air the one Sunday, and I the following week. From his remarks it seemed that Mr. Williamson was more than satisfied with the way I piloted the meeting. Yet when he came back I was never asked, literally never once, to lead. Mr. Williamson was getting old. We would go down to the open-air, expecting him to lead, but would hear him say, "George, I am not feeling too bright tonight, you take charge."

Then, something would snap inside me. I would feel like walking up to Mr. Williamson and saying, "If you ask this fellow George again, and don't ask me, that will be the end. You won't see me again." I am so grateful to the Lord for so graciously giving me victory, so that never, as far as I know, did I ever betray the feelings within, by the slightest action or even by the tone of my voice. No one, not my most intimate fellow-workers, not even my fiancée guessed what a storm was raging in my breast. I had victory but not freedom (John 8:36). It was this deliverance that I really needed; for every time that jealousy raised its ugly head within, it brought a horrible cloud between the Master and my little soul.

Hudson Taylor once said: "A trip across the sea will make no one a missionary", and my promotion to the status of "full-time worker" did not deal with the conflict within. The selfishness of my heart, with its accompanying pride and jealousy, pursued me into the Africa Evangelistic Band. In my unsaved days I could never play "second fiddle". I always had to be captain of the cricket or football team, and I found that this spirit was still present.

Unless I was the "star-turn" at a convention I was miserable. The first year in the A.E.B. it seemed as if Mr. von Staden valued my work more than the other Pilgrims, and I basked in the sunshine of his favour. The next year (1941), however, Brother G. came to the Transvaal, and achieved success far surpassing anything to which I could lay claim. It was a very bitter pill for me to swallow. I remember Brother G.'s coming to the Transvaal Headquarters. He explained, "I have come to fetch the big tent. I commenced in a house, but we were quickly crowded out. I had fortunately brought the small tent and that was filled in a few days. The first time I made an appeal there, half the congregation stood up to seek the Lord."

I tried to say, "Praise the Lord." That was the proper response, I knew, yet I was so conscious that there was bitterness and rebellion in my heart. Why should this man get the crowds, while I was fortunate if I got twenty or thirty at my meetings, with one or two seekers? Then to make matters worse, Mr. von Staden sent me to work a tent campaign with Brother G. Our kind hostess (and she was kind) would be loud in her praise of my fellow-worker. Wasn't Mr. G. wonderful tonight," she would come and whisper to me. Never a word of appreciation for me! How I *wanted* to say: "Mrs. S., let me tell you a few things about Mr. G., then you wouldn't think so much of him." Oh! praise the Lord for keeping my mouth shut. But praise the Lord still more for the day when I trusted the Lord to deal with the cause of "evil speaking".

In August, 1942, after our honeymoon, we were sent to the Eastern Cape. Our Superintendent, a great soul-winner, greeted us with tremendous optimism. He almost seemed to think that we were "bringing revival in our suit-cases"; though why, I do not know. We had meetings in important churches, good attendances throughout, but we "caught nothing". This was literally true. After five months of evangelising—not a single soul, not one! This was repeated in Port Elizabeth where we had a series of tent campaigns. It was the time of the "Black Out" (due to war conditions), and I would walk the dark streets, 11.00 p.m., midnight, 1.00 a.m., crying to the Lord for power. I would be up again at 4.00 a.m., my usual hour in those days for commencing the "Morning Watch". How my body stood the strain I do not know.

We concluded 1942 with a "Special Yuletide Campaign", conducted from Christmas Day to New Year's Eve. Again no fish! Our Superintendent asked a well-known minister to preach at the final service. He brought a mighty message, and then made an appeal. As all our heads were bowed my heart was saying, "I hope no one raises his hand. If someone does what will they think of me? They will say, 'Friend preached a whole week, and no results. This man comes and the first night he gets souls.' " There was no response to the appeal, but, as I groped my way through the Black Out to my lodgings, I felt like a murderer. I knew some of the people who had been in that service, knew that they needed salvation desperately, yet I wanted them to go to Hell to save my reputation.

When we returned to Cape Town and the Headquarters of the A.E.B. we decided to hand in our resignations. The excuse we gave was that our first baby was on the way. The real reason, however, was, at least as far as I was concerned, that we felt a total failure. In those days you did not talk to the opposite sex about babies to be. Babsie, therefore, went to Miss Garratt, and I to one of the Superintendents. The latter seemed quite ready to accept our resignation. Perhaps, he, too, felt that we were failures. Dear Miss Garratt would not hear of it. In her Irish way she said: "Dear Babsie, we would not even think of it. When we accepted you and Bertram, we took account of the fact that you might have children."

In March, 1943, I went to the monthly meeting of the "Victorious Life Testimony". The Rev. Kenneth Bedwell was preaching on Gal. 2:20. Like a flash of light from the sky this realisation burst upon me: "For months you have been praying for power, but what do you really need?" A leader of camp-meetings in America became so tired of the same people coming back year after year for the "fulness" that finally he cried out, "What you people need is not the filling but the killing." From that moment I no longer sought the Lord for power, but for crucifixion. When the Lord saw that I was on the right track He graciously began to give us souls. From that time onwards we had genuine seekers in every campaign. Yet I myself was not yet through into the experience.

In July, 1943, I went up to Windhoek, the capital of what used to be "German South West Africa", to be one of the two chief speakers at a convention of the A.E.B. held in the Methodist Church there. The series of meetings commenced on a Thursday, and was planned for ten days. Right throughout I felt as flat as a pancake on which an elephant had sat. I said to myslf, "All the money they spent to bring me here (it was a 1,000 mile train-journey) was wasted." Fortunately my fellow-labourer was dear Mr. H. T. de Villiers, "a man full of faith and the Holy Ghost, mighty in the Scriptures", and his ministry saved the convention.

By the Wednesday I was utterly desperate. I went out into the fields, determined to seek the Lord until He met me. I got nowhere, however, and, at last, utterly dispirited, crept into bed. The following evening I was sitting in front of the hall while the Chairman of the convention conducted community singing. I do not know if it was a remark he made, or a line in one of the choruses, but suddenly there came a second flash of Heavenly light. It spoke thus to my heart, "All these months you have been seeking God for crucifixion, but you don't really believe He can do it." If, before that revealing moment, you had inquired, "Do you really think the Lord can deliver you from selfishness and pride and jealousy?", I would have replied, "Why do you ask? Of course I do. That is what I preach." But that night I saw my "evil heart of unbelief" (Heb. 3:12). While my lips had been crying, "Oh! God, deliver me from this accursed self", my heart had been replying: "But, Lord, I know you can't do it. You see, Lord, I'm a Baker" (my mother's maiden name).

My mother had thirteen brothers and sisters, and it seemed as if they were all the domineering type. They all had to be "No. 1". They were always right and the other man or woman was wrong. It seems awful to so slander your own family. Yet, unless I am frank, you will find it difficult to understand my problem. When I realised that I had been saying in unbelief, "I was born a Baker; I will die a Baker. I cannot be anything different", I realised why for weeks and months I had been praying in vain. "Let not that man" (the doubter) "think that he shall receive anything from the Lord" (Jas. 1:7, Revised Version).

The next evening was Friday. I was due to bring the main message, but I went to the Chairman and asked: "Would you mind if I just gave a few, short opening remarks?" He readily gave his consent. I have forgotten my exact words, but I said in effect, "Friends, for a week I have been preaching holiness and the victorious life, but I do not experience it myself. My heart is full of selfishness, pride, and jealousy. Please pray for me." I have often asked myself, "Was it necessary for me to strip my soul naked in that way?" I think one should be very cautious in a matter of this sort. I am afraid public confessions have been made which have only brought embarrassment to the hearers, and unfortunate consequences to the one who made them. Yet to this day I believe that this baring of my inner soul was the will of God.

Up to that point the pride of my heart had produced hypocrisy. I so much wanted people to think well of me, that I was quite willing for them to have an inflated opinion of me. For instance in my early days in the A.E.B. dear Mr. von Staden would tell the friends, "Mr. Friend has made great sacrifices to enter this work. He has given up his splendid position in the commercial world to become a poor Pilgrim." I think Mr. von Staden was judging my past in business life by the size of the car in which I was driving round. I should have gone to him and said, "Mr. von Staden, I had a good job in Cape Town, but not nearly as wonderful as you think." To hear these flattering remarks, however, gave a big boost to my ego. I, therefore, did not correct these false impressions and was thus, again, guilty of "making a lie" (Rev. 21:27). But the fact that, on that Friday night, I was so honest about my condition, enabled God to pour His reality into my soul.

The immediate result of that confession was, however, just the very reverse of all I had expected. I had thought, "Now that I have so humbled myself, even into the dust, I will waken up tomorrow to find myself deluged with Divine blessing." Instead on the Saturday morning I felt as dead as the chair on which I sat. It seemed as if I had lost every scrap of religion I ever possessed; and as if God Himself had turned His back on me. For years I could not understand why, after obeying God, I should feel so utterly forsaken until one day it suddenly dawned upon me: Well, of course, the Lord was knocking every prop out from under me, so that I would have nothing upon which I could lean but the naked Word of God.

The workers and speakers at this convention met together each morning for Bible study and united prayer, but I felt too miserable that Saturday to join them. I went down to the Town Gardens and did something which was always a great comfort to me; I wrote a letter to my wife. When this rather lengthy epistle was concluded I looked at my watch: "Just time enough to post this letter and make my way home for lunch." When, however, I arrived at the house I found it open, but deserted. They had all been invited out for lunch but I was not there to tell. When they returned they were very sorry for me. "My, what you have missed! We had a wonderful meal!"

Yet, to my dying day, I will be profoundly grateful for the lost lunch. I first of all prepared a little for the afternoon meeting at which I had to speak, and then discovered that I still had twenty minutes to spare before I needed to walk down to the Methodist Church. In some way, I cannot remember now how, my attention was directed to II Cor. 5:14, 15 as it is translated in the Revised Version. I noticed two things in that passage: first of all that the Lord Jesus had died on the Cross; not only to deliver us from Hell (praise the Lord for that marvellous redemption), but there was something even more in His precious Blood for us. "He died for all, that they that live should no longer live unto themselves, but unto Him Who for their sakes died and rose again."

This is wonderful, I thought: I can be so really, so radically delivered from all selfishness that I will never again "live unto myself, but unto Him"; all my desiring and doing will arise from selfless love for the Master and men. I saw a second fact: "We thus judge, that if one died for all, therefore all died" (II Cor. 5:14). I said: "All! Why, that includes me." Immediately I began to praise the Lord. At first it was just "a work" (John 6:29), i.e. a sheer act of the will. I had to make myself praise, for all my feelings were utterly against me.

If at that moment you had asked, "How do you feel?", I would have replied, "Feel? I feel awful. I feel as if I am going to Hell." Yet I walked up and down my little room saying, "Lord, I thank Thee that when You died, I died with You." As I did so, suddenly I knew it was real. Praise the Lord for His marvellous grace, and praise the Lord that from that day to this I have been able to say with truth and certainty, "I am crucified with Christ" (Gal. 2:20). Yet that assurance has only been mine because the initial faith of that first moment has been repeated day by day; because each morning, and in each test, I have "delivered up myself unto death" (II Cor. 4:11).

This is, of course, not physical death, for it is "we who live" or, as it is in the original Greek, "we, the living ones" who are "delivered". For instance, there have been times when I have been pushed into the background, and a younger man advanced to the position that might have seemed mine by right. Or, another worker has been used, while I seemed to have been laid on the shelf. At such moments the Devil has been quick to come and say, "You are the old Friend. Inside, you are just as jealous as ever." But the Holy Spirit, in His tender love, has shown me how to combat the Tempter. At that crucial moment I have cried, sometimes in the silence of my soul on a public platform or in a crowded congregation, "Lord, I thank Thee that when Thou didst die, I died with Thee." And how quickly the Holy Spirit has responded to the faith of my heart with the renewed assurance that I was still "crucified".

At other times it has just been the reverse. The Lord has been pleased to use me, and "The Accuser of the Brethren" (Rev. 12:10) has come with his insinuation, "You are just like you used to be, all puffed up inside." As I have pleaded the power of the Cross I have once again been conscious that the only reaction to God's gracious using of me, has been humble gratitude. Praise His Wonderful Name!

CHAPTER 10

ONE morning in 1946, when we were working in the Province of Natal and living in Durban, I went to Babsie and said, "Darling, for almost a year now I have had a strong conviction that the Lord wants us to go to Britain." Babsie's reply was very squashing: "Nonsense, there's more than enough work to do in South Africa." That was the end of the matter, at least for twelve months. I then ventured to go back to Babsie: "My darling, I can't get rid of that urge to go to Britain. Is it not from the Lord?" Babsie, however, had not changed in the slightest: "You can go to Britain, but you will have to go on your own. I will take the children and go to my mother."

I was the "spare wheel" of the A.E.B., and we had been sent to Natal to take the place of the district superintendent, who was going to England, for a six months' furlough. Owing to travelling difficulties and other circumstances, he was away two and one-half years. The Council of the A.E.B., therefore, decided that we should "stay put", and that the other superintendent should be appointed to a new district which they were anxious to open up. Babsie and I, of course, accepted the decision of the Council as the will of God. Babsie, I think, must have been very relieved because we would have to remain in Natal for, at the very least, the next six years, and her husband would have to give up "his strange idea of wanting to go to Britain."

At this time I went down to Bloemfontein, "The Central City" of South Africa, to conduct special services for Christians. To my surprise the other superintendent walked into one of these meetings (he was passing through Bloemfontein). After the service, we went for a walk. Although he, too, had accepted the decision of the Council, I could see from a remark he made that both he and his wife felt, in their innermost beings, that Natal was still the Lord's place for them. I at once said, "Babsie and I will be most happy to have you come back to your old district." This was just the assurance this dear worker for God needed. He approached the Council and they gave their consent for him to be reinstated in his old position.

Babsie and I went back, and went back very gladly, to being "spare wheel" again—very useful articles. Thus it was that when the doctor said, "Captain Dobbie must get away from the wet Cape winter and have a complete change", the Council had someone whom they could send to the Bible College to take his place temporarily, as "Acting Principal".

One afternoon in August, 1948, while we were there, Babsie came to me: "I was having such a blessed time of fellowship with the Lord, telling Him how much I loved Him and how ready I was to go anywhere and do anything He wanted when suddenly, like a bolt from the blue, the Master asked me: 'If that is so, what about going to Britain?' I was full of excuses: 'Lord, they have rationing over there. The country is still recovering from the ravages of war. We have no relatives there, no home, and we have small children. Where will we get the money to travel so far?' But finally I said, 'Lord, if this is Your plan for us, I am willing to go'."

Some weeks after this dear Miss Bazeley who was, at that time, one of the two "Lady Superintendents" of the Bible College said to me, "When your wife first mentioned the possibility of your going to Britain I was very much opposed to it but the more I pray about it the more I feel that it is of God." This, coming from such a saint, was a great encouragement. And yet? Yet, who in Britain would ever want a little unknown Pilgrim from South Africa?

During the short Spring vacation of the Bible College I went to speak at a camp convention. While there, I received a letter asking if I could not come to speak at the A.E.B. Convention in Durban. I wrote back, thanking them for their "gracious invitation", but explaining that unfortunately I could not come as I was expected back at "Glenvar" for a further three months in the Bible College.

This arrangement was, however, suddenly altered for, while still at the camp convention, an order came from the Council, directing me to go immediately to Pretoria as the district superintendent there had had a serious breakdown, and they needed help urgently. However, after a few weeks there, I found my presence was no longer needed. I, therefore, wrote to say that, if they still wanted me, I could now come to Durban.

In the meantime, however, they had been able to secure the services of the well-known Major Allister Smith so that I was no longer needed. As he prayed about the matter, the district superintendent felt more and more certain that he should do what he had never done before—have two chief speakers. It was, therefore, arranged that I should give the Bible readings in the afternoon and that Major Allister Smith should be the preacher in the evenings.

One day, as we were having tea together between the two sessions, that great warrior for God leaned over and said in the most matter-of-fact tones, "Brother, I would like to get you to Britain. Can you come this summer?" I was thunderstruck, but I managed to whisper quietly (for we were surrounded by people): "Major, I have felt led in that direction and, if you feel this to be the will of God, I am willing." The Major then added, "I will write to some of the leaders in Britain and suggest that they invite you. You need not worry about the expenses. They will be responsible for these."

Later on we discussed the matter more fully. I could see that the dear Major was somewhat taken aback when he heard that I had a wife and two small children. I think, if I may say so, that, had he known that I was married, he would not have suggested my going to Britain.

He must, however, have felt that it was too late to withdraw and he wrote to three leaders. From the one he never got a reply. The second gentleman approached, wrote very sympathetically but said that his organisation could not commit themselves to such a venture. The third was a characteristically gracious letter from the Rev. Maynard James. He wrote somewhat to this effect: "I am so sorry that we cannot offer to pay the travelling expenses. We have just opened a new Bible College, and all our available funds have gone into that. If, however, Brother Friend feels that he can come in faith, we will be glad to use him at our Whitsuntide Convention, towards the end of May, and again at our Sheffield Convention in September."

When this letter arrived on December 16th, 1948 (I remember the date so well) I felt, "This is from the Lord." My wife still had many doubts but her husband seemed to be so certain that she agreed to accompany me to Cape Town where we made enquiries about the possibility of a passage to England. Shipping was still feeling the effects of the war and we drew a blank everywhere with the single exception of the Union Castle Company. They said, "All our ships are fully booked up but if you are willing to travel austerity, we could offer you a place on the 'Arundel Castle', which is due to leave Cape Town on March 25th, 1949. She was a troopcarrier during the war, and this will be her last trip before she is converted back to a passenger-ship. Would you be willing to be separated, your wife and children to go in a large dormitory with forty or eighty other ladies, and you to go in with the men?"

We asked: "Can we have time to consider it?"

They replied: "There is very little accommodation left on this ship and we advise you to decide today."

We said, "We will let you know in an hour's time."

We hurried round the corner, found a quiet lane in the heart of the city and there we cried unto the Lord, "Dear Master, show us what we should do." If we travelled on the "Arundel" we would arrive in England six weeks before the Whitsuntide Convention. Even if enough came in to pay our passage, was there not the danger that we should find ourselves in a strange country with nowhere to go, and no money to pay hotel expenses? Then after the May meetings, there was a space of more than three months with not a single engagement. With only two invitations was it not the height of folly to leave the security of our own land and a settled position in the A.E.B.? After prayer, however, we decided to trust God for the impossible, and went back to the Union Castle: "We have decided to accept your offer of a passage on the 'Arundel'."

We paid our deposit money and then came the tests! One deeply spiritual lady who knew England well said, "I don't think you should take the children with you. Is there not someone with whom you could leave them?" Mr. Clothier, one of our district superintendents, came to me very worried: "Bertram, you must first have a place where you can go and stay in England before you can think of leaving South Africa. It is exceedingly difficult to find accommodation there" (he had just returned from a furlough in Britain). "I wish I could invite you to stay with my parents but my two brothers have both recently married, and they are living there now. They could not get rooms anywhere."

When we reached Britain we saw the reason for Mr. Clothier's concern. Because of the widespread destruction, which had resulted from the air-raids, there was a desperate shortage of housing, and the Government had instituted a points' system. For instance: if you had served in the British Forces you gained so many points. Points were also allocated according to the number of years you had been in the area, and so on. We would have been at the bottom of every list, with a faint possibility of getting accommodation, if we were fortunate, after three or four years. We also met quite a lot of just, but severe criticism. One Council member said, "Britain is taking our one ewe lamb" (II Samuel 12:3). One of the district superintendents asked, "Bertram, why on earth do you want to go to England. They have more preachers than they know what to do with. They are falling over each other."

Yet the Lord, in His matchless grace, created sympathy and

support in hearts. We received a letter from a dear couple in the Transvaal, whom we scarcely knew (we had only met them at conventions), "We have heard that you have been appointed to work on the Rand. (The 'Rand' is Johannesburg and the cities around it.) We have felt led to send you £120.00 to cover your house rent for a year." Today the equivalent of £120.00 would scarcely be enough for two months, so colossal has been the inflation. We wrote back thanking them very much for their most generous gift but explaining that we were now going to Britain. We, therefore, returned the cheque, never expecting to see it again. We thought that this lady and gentleman, like most of our friends, would feel that we were making a big mistake.

After a few weeks, however, the cheque came back to us, as large as ever! The covering letter explained why: "After prayer, we felt that we should make this contribution to your travelling expenses as a small expression of our gratitude to Britain, for all the spiritual gifts she has sent to South Africa—for the preachers, the missionaries, the books, the hymns she has given this land."

We felt that we ought to settle with the "Union Castle" on the third Thursday of February. We were living some distance from Cape Town and had to go into the City on that date to speak at a meeting. We still needed, however, another £51.00 to cover the balance owing on our passage-money. On the Tuesday we received a letter from one of the banks, asking us to call at their Cape Town office, as they had a mail-transfer for us from Natal. We said to each other: "We must not get too excited. It is probably only for £3.00 or £5.00. Anyhow we will be most grateful for that amount. It will certainly help."

You can, therefore, guess how great was our amazement and gratitude when we found that the mail-transfer was for £53.00! With what joy and triumph we marched down from the Bank to the Union Castle offices, and handed the complete amount over the counter. As she did so, my wife said to the clerk: "Sir, this sum is an answer to prayer." He seemed really impressed and we trust that that little testimony brought eternal blessing to his soul.

He also had wonderful news for us. Instead of being squeezed in with forty or eighty other passengers we had been given a four-berth cabin in an ideal situation, right amidships on the main deck. Why we should have got that, I do not know but the Lord loves to spoil His children!

As we stood on the deck of the "Arundel Castle", gazing down at the relatives and friends who had come to bid us farewell (visitors were not allowed on board, I think, because the old troop-ship regulations were still in force), Mr. H. G. Semark, the greatly beloved General Superintendent of the A.E.B., shouted up: "Have you read the portion for today in Daily Light?"

Amongst the other texts for March 25th we read these words: "And behold, I am with thee, and will keep thee in all places whither thou goest and will bring thee again into this land; for I will not leave thee, until I have done that which I have spoken to thee of" (Gen. 28:15). How marvellously this promise was fulfilled! We had an unusually pleasant trip. We slept very well. We experienced practically no sea-sickness, and had many opportunities for personal work. I was also privileged to take two services on board, one of which was attended by the Captain himself.

As we were returning from our day ashore at Las Palmas, Babsie was intrigued by the fascinating dolls displayed for sale at the quay-side. "Can't we buy one of the smaller ones for Alice?" (our little three year-old daughter). The hard-hearted father replied, "No, Alice has playthings; we can't waste the Lord's money." As we came across still more dolls the plaintive plea was repeated: "Daddy, can't we buy one?" But all Mummy got was an unrelenting "No".

With a sad heart she climbed on board but as I was returning to our cabin from the bathroom, I heard a lady's voice down the passage: "Mr. Friend, I have been looking for you." She was a Christian from Dr. Alan Redpath's church at Richmond and had attended the services I took. "Would your little daughter like this doll?" She handed me a lovely doll much larger than the one Babsie had thought of buying.

"How good is the God we adore,
Our faithful, unchangeable Friend."

The "Arundel Castle" pulled into Southampton Docks early on the Saturday just before Easter. We sailed through the Immigration and Customs. My wife's face seemed to be the guarantee that there was no "hokey-pokey business", and by 11.00 a.m. we were well on our way to Lancashire for our first services in Britain which were to take place the next day, for, before we ever left Cape Town we were fully booked up (with the exception of one week) for six months. The two engagements, which launched us on our gipsy wanderings overseas, so mushroomed that we were kept busy all over Britain for four years. The Lord marvellously met our need of accommodation. We literally did not spend five minutes looking for a place in which to stay. As soon as we had to leave one dwelling another was offered; often without the person's doing so knowing we had to move. Philippians 4:19 was so abundantly fulfilled that we never had a moment's financial anxiety. Yet more than all these temporal blessings, rich though they were, was the sense of the Master's Presence. The Lord so made His "Behold, I am with thee" (Gen. 28 : 15) a conscious reality that His nearness is the outstanding memory of those forty-eight months in Britain. To everyone of His trusting, clinging children He is still "Immanuel—God with us" (Matthew 1 : 23).

CHAPTER 11

ALL AUTHORITY IS GIVEN UNTO ME
(Matt. 28:18)

WE returned to South Africa towards the end of March, 1953, and for the next seven years I worked as a kind of "Spiritual Special", taking part in conventions and evangelistic campaigns. For most of this time my wife, for the sake of our children, had to stay at home. During the school-holidays, however, Babsie often accompanied me to meetings, where her ministry was much appreciated, as she is a most acceptable speaker.

Then in January, 1960, we were transferred to Rhodesia to take charge of the A.E.B. work in that country and Zambia. There we were "in journeyings often" (II Corinthians 11:26); often on lonely roads, 200 miles or more from the nearest garage. If, therefore, I had had mechanical problems I would have been in a very tight corner indeed, for what I know of the inside of a car could be written on the back of a postage stamp. The Lord was, however, so good to me. Only once did I have any trouble in all the many thousands of miles I travelled; and that was when an ex-motor-mechanic was with me. In spite of the rough roads I sometimes had to traverse, I never even had a puncture.

Then in January, 1966, three letters arrived almost simultaneously: one from Australia, one from Britain, and one from Japan. My wife said immediately, "This is the call of God. Our children's schooling is completed. They are both in good jobs. The Lord has freed me from all home responsibilities to accompany you." I did not share her conviction; at least not to the same extent. Even after we had written to say that we would come, I was oppressed by many doubts.

All through 1966, while we were still working in Rhodesia, my mind was once again an awful battle-ground. Were we not stepping out of the will of God? Did not our children still need us? It was true that they were well equipped, both financially and mentally, to look after themselves, but would they not backslide in our absence? On two occasions we went with Reginald and Alice to see a Billy Graham film, in which the central figure was a high school boy, who was "going to the dogs" because his parents were too busy with their career to give him the attention he needed. Were we not about to commit the same crime?

This dread was increased by a dream I had about that time. I was hurrying on my way to a meeting when, most unexpectedly, I came across Alice. She greeted me with a careless giggle. To my horror I saw that she was surrounded by companions of the most undesirable sort. I yearned to give myself back to my neglected daughter; to lay at her feet the love and attention she was now seeking in the society of these loose-living girls and boys. I looked at my watch. Alas! I was already late. I had to rush off to my meeting—a meeting for which I was selling the soul of my child.

This dream lived with me for many weeks. I kept asking myself: "Is this not a warning from God?" This question came with renewed emphasis when one day Reginald said to us, "When you leave I will go all to pieces." More than once I was on the point of going to my typewriter, and sending off three letters, cancelling our visits to those countries, but each time something, I knew not what, held me back.

Thus, one morning in November 1966, Babsie and I found ourselves driving out of the gate of the house which had been our home for nearly seven years. Alice had moved into her own flat. Boarding had been arranged for Reginald. The work would be in the hands of a very capable district superintendent who had been appointed to take our place. Yet there was an ache in our hearts which no words could describe. I said to Babsie: "We are saying 'good-bye' to our family life."

One morning we heard over the radio the voice of the announcer: "The Qantas pilots have gone on strike." We pricked up our ears for we were booked on a Qantas (The Australian Government Air Line) flight. Then we said to each other, "Oh, we do not need to worry. We have got more than a month before we are due to fly on December 19th and such strikes usually last only a week."

The week, however, became two, and the two three, and the three a month. While I remained behind in Rhodesia, Babsie went down to South Africa with Alice to say 'good-bye' to her relatives. I got an anxious telegram from her: "Please consult travel agent regarding flight. Can get no information here." I went to the agency and they promised to make exhaustive enquiries. When I returned they said, "We have asked everywhere and no one can tell us anything. The other airlines are just as much in the dark as we are."

I flew down to South Africa on Friday, December 16th and met my wife in Pretoria. Babsie explained: "The reason I sent that telegram is that I have tried all the Qantas offices in the Republic and I only get one answer: 'We can do nothing for you. Our pilots are on strike. We have asked travel agencies throughout the world to request their clients to make other arrangements'!" However, hope dies hard in the human breast and I made one final attempt on the Saturday morning. I phoned the Qantas Headquarters in South Africa, but alas, in vain! I told them that I simply had to be in Sydney by December 26th but the only reply they could give was: "We are very sorry, but we are helpless. Our pilots have tied our hands."

They had, however, a suggestion to make: "Why don't you try South African Airways? They also have a direct flight to Australia." So off we went to our last hope. The S.A. Airways were very courteous and sympathetic, but they also were unable to help us. "All our flights are fully booked right up to February. Would you be willing to fly to Rome? We might be able to get seats on a plane from there to Sydney."

This would have added another 12,000 miles to the distance and would probably have increased the fare by 200 per cent, which would have been far beyond all our financial resources. However, as a gesture of despair I asked them to work out the extra cost and said I would be back on Monday morning.

It was two very dejected people who stood in the rain, near the centre of Pretoria, waiting for a bus. Suddenly Babsie turned to me: "Do you hear that?" I listened; heard nothing. "What is it, my darling?"

"From somewhere over the road I hear the notes of that hymn:
'Be not dismayed, whate'er betide,
God will take care of you.'"

It came to Babsie as a very personal word from the Master Himself, and all her gloom fled. Our wonderfully kind hosts in Pretoria, Mr. and Mrs. Albert Brandt, who were to take our places in Rhodesia but who were then still working in Transvaal, however, concluded that our way was completely blocked. Mr. Brandt said, half teasingly, half seriously: "Now you can come and help me with my Christmas convention."

Sunday morning early, I was having my quiet time in the lounge when the Lord Himself spoke to me through Matt. 28:18, 19: "All authority is given unto me in heaven and in earth, go ye therefore." I noticed that the Greek word translated "go" could be rendered with equal accuracy "travel". "Travel therefore" came with all the authority of a Divine command. I cannot tell you with what certainty I knew that this was no wishful thinking but the very Voice of the Master Himself.

All those agonising months in 1966 I had said over and over again, "Lord, you said: 'My sheep hear my voice . . . and they follow me,' (John 10 : 27), Lord, I am as ignorant as a stupid sheep. I do not know which way to turn, but you will not leave me to grope bewildered along an unknown path."

At last, through the darkness had come that glorious Voice, sought so long. In a moment all frustration and anxiety fled. Outwardly everything was just as dark and dismal as ever, but I had changed. I dashed into the bedroom where Babsie was praying: "Look! This is what the Lord has told me." She embraced the word and began to pack just as if we were certain of a place on the plane—or rather, because we WERE certain.

Thus on Monday morning, December 19th, we stepped into "Jan Smuts Airport", carried our suitcases up to the counter and said, "We have come to catch the 9.00 a.m. Qantas flight to Sydney." The young lady did not know what to make of us. I wonder if she thought she had to deal with two escaped lunatics? She called another official. I still remember his name—a Mr. Laubscher. I wish I could describe the blank bewilderment on his face. In a tone of utter amazement he said, "But there are no Qantas flights. Look up there. On the first floor are the Qantas offices. They have been closed for weeks."

"But we MUST get to Sydney."

I think, just to get rid of us as quickly as possible, they agreed to call the Qantas people once again on the phone. They called us back to the counter: "The Qantas people say we can send you via London and they will foot the bill!"

In the meantime a tall, handsome gentleman made his appearance at the counter and listened with manifest interest. Finally he asked, "Won't you come and sit at these coffee tables? Who are you, and what are you going to do in Australia?"

After some minutes conversation he called the official and ordered, "Mr. Laubscher, please get Mr. and Mrs. Friend off today."

We asked in some surprise, "Sir, who are you?"

He replied: "I am the head of the passenger department of South African Airways."

A little later Mr. Laubscher brought us brand new tickets— "Johannesburg-London. London-Sydney" saying, "We will put you on a S.A. Airways plane leaving 'Jan Smuts' at 7.00 p.m. tonight, and will telex B.O.A.C. asking them to book you on one of their planes to Sydney."

That evening, just as we were going into the Departure Lounge for the final formalities, Mr. Brandt came dashing up: "This plane touches down in Salisbury. I will call your children on the phone and ask them to meet you." In those days a trunk call took about forty-five minutes but Mr. Brandt got through almost immediately. The lady with whom our son was boarding, said, "I am so sorry, but Reginald is right on the other side of town. He has gone to see his girl friend. I will try and contact him." She did. "I am sorry. Reginald is out. He has gone for a walk with his lady-love."

When Reginald did eventually return, he was greeted with the words: "Your parents' plane will be at the airport in 15 minutes' time." That meant a trip of twelve miles in almost as many minutes. Reginald dived into his car and, I presume, broke the speed-limit in his new G.T. Cortina! On the way, however, he called at Alice's flat. She was out. He left a note on her door. She returned a few minutes later, saw the message, and began to cry. Just at that moment a young Portuguese happened to pass. He could hardly speak English, but he saw her distress, and asked, "What's the matter?"

"My parents are at the Airport, and I haven't a car." In his broken English he said: "I take in my car." Down they went along the wide road to the Airport in this kind stranger's big Mercedes. I don't think Alice ever met him again, but he was truly to her "an angel from Heaven".

In the meantime, our plane had been delayed at 'Jan Smuts' and arrived 30 minutes late at Salisbury. Thus, as we stepped from the long corridor into the Airport Concourse there were our children waiting to meet us. How our eyes feasted on them! Would we ever see them again? Yet the pang of parting was eased by the assurance that we were moving in the will of God.

We touched down at Heathrow Airport in London at about 2.30 on Tuesday afternoon, December 20th, and immediately made our way to the B.O.A.C. office: "Yes, we did get the telex from Johannesburg but, you know, there is a Qantas strike and all our planes are fully booked up. The demand for seats has been so great that even the waiting lists have been closed. We suggest that you stand in the queue tomorrow. There's always the possibility of a cancellation and you might get a place on an All-India plane and then from there to Sydney. Or, if not, on Thursday there is a flight to Hong Kong and you might get a place on it."

I whispered to Babsie: "Let's go. I do not believe this is the way the Lord does things." On the bus I explained to Babsie, "I have a strong urge to go to the B.O.A.C. Headquarters at Victoria." The official there said: "All our planes to Australia are fully booked but I'll try." He phoned "Reservations". As he listened his eyes became wider and wider. He came back to us: "You know what has happened? Two seats on Friday's plane have just become vacant. We will put you on that flight and you should arrive on Sunday morning in Sydney."

Now we had to find inexpensive accommodation for the three days we were to spend in London. We remembered that Mrs. Rush, widow of Percy Rush, author of "Is This Not a Brand?", had a Christian guest house at Kennington Oval. At about 5.30 p.m. we knocked at her door. Mrs. Rush greeted us with the words, "Shouldn't you be in Australia?"

This great little lady (only about 94 pounds), 80 years of age, while on a preaching tour six months previously, had stayed in our home in Salisbury and knew our plans. We replied, "Please let us first come in out of the cold and then we can explain." Mrs. Rush then countered with: "I must explain before you do. If you had come this morning, I would have been forced to turn you away for I simply had no room. At about 11.00 a.m. today I got a phone call from a couple, saying that their plans had been unexpectedly changed. There is, therefore, on the third floor a room all ready with the beds made up; you can move in there straight away."

While in Pretoria we got a phone call inviting us to a prayer-meeting of the supporters of the "Japan Mission for Hospital Evangelisation". While there, we heard that our great friends, Neil and Peggy Verwey, Founders and Leaders of this Mission, had just arrived in England. Mrs. Rush was able to give us the phone number of someone who was acquainted with the Verweys. We called him on the phone: "Yes, I *can* tell you where the Verweys are. They have a meeting tonight in Dorset, but are due in London tomorrow. This is their phone number."

It was such a thrill to hear Neil's voice the next morning. He and Peggy were like brother and sister to Babsie and me. They had treated me with amazing kindness during my two visits to Japan in 1956 and 1962 and we had enjoyed rich fellowship with them during their deputation tour in Rhodesia. Neil said, "We are only a few minutes away from you. We will be around in a quarter of an hour."

When they arrived Neil characteristically asked: "Where would you like us to take you?" I replied: "We only want to be with you. Just take us round London." When, however, they persisted, Babsie ventured, "Could we not go and see Colin and Joy Molyneux?" They were the much loved Directors of the A.E.B. work in the Congo (now known as Zaire). Their eldest child, Colin, was like a brother to Reginald and a son to Babsie and me.

I objected: "No: it's too far. It's in Surrey". Peggy, however, who was the navigator (Neil was the pilot) looked up her maps. "It's only about fifteen miles from here." The Pilot said, "We'll go there."

As we braked to a halt before 5 Langton Avenue, Ewell, another car pulled up in front of us and four young fellows, followed by two or three girls, tumbled out. One of them came to find out who was in the car behind. It was young Colin. No, he didn't recognise the driver. But who was that sitting at the back? The face seemed so familiar but it couldn't be, of course. His eyes must be playing him tricks, for the person he thought it was, was far away in Rhodesia.

Then Colin realised that he was not "seeing things", and burst out with: "Oh! Mr. Friend, where have you come from?" What a gathering of the ransomed! All four of their sons were as keen as mustard for the Lord (they had no daughters); all of them are today in whole-time missionary work. Malcolm, the second eldest, said: "This is one of the very rare occasions in which we have all been together as a family" (the children were so scattered). The Lord gave us the privilege of sharing that joy with our friends: but for the Qantas strike it would never have been ours (Rom. 8: 28).

Thus on Sunday morning our B.O.A.C. Boeing jet rose from the ground for the last lap of its journey, when suddenly Babsie felt the window at her side growing strangely hot. She looked out and saw that the metal plate, which guarded the light which flashed on and off in flight, had become loosened. It was flapping wildly in the wind, banging itself against the wing, and leaving the electric wires dangerously exposed. Babsie realised that at any moment a stray spark might explode the petrol tanks, housed in the wings. Very considerately she did not tell her husband what she had seen but she pleaded the word on which the Master had caused us to hope, "Lord, Thou hast said, 'All authority is given to me'. You would not have brought us so far, and then left us to die in the sky."

As we stepped out of the plane at Sydney we saw the ground crew gazing up at that gaping wound in the wing. We were glad that our Boeing was going to get expert attention.

Yet, how grateful we were that a mightier Hand than theirs had guarded that danger-spot and brought us to our desired haven just twenty-four hours before our first engagement in "The Land of the Kangaroo".

CHAPTER 12

WE had gone to Australia in response to only one invitation, i.e. to the New South Wales Keswick Convention. This hardly seemed to justify so long a journey and so great an expense. We trusted the Lord, however, to open other doors, and He graciously honoured that faith, giving us opportunities for ministry in three of the five Australian states, and for a period of eight months until we had to leave for our first engagement in Britain. At first it seemed as if our united ministry would be wrecked upon the rock of my dear wife's physical condition. For twenty years she had suffered from migraine headaches. She had consulted doctors and specialists, tried many medicines, was X-rayed from head to foot. Nothing helped. She got slowly worse. Every fortnight the attacks would return, and poor Babsie would have to shut herself up in her room for two or three days of misery. This was possible when we had a home of our own but not now when we were continually changing residence, and there were meetings for both of us around every corner.

One Sunday morning in March, 1967, Babsie dragged herself out of bed, and wended her weary way to the suburban station. The service in front of us was a nightmare to her. Then, as Babsie sat beside me in the crowded train, the Lord graciously met with her. He reminded her of how twenty-five years before, as a young Pilgrim, she had cried unto Him for her physical need and He had sent immediate deliverance. When, however, five years later the migraine visited her, she turned from Him to human aids.

I heard no voice but in the silence of her soul my wife at my side cried in agony: "Oh! Lord, I have rejected You." Babsie was to testify later: "As the train turned the bend to cross a little brook, I confessed the unbelief of my heart (Hebrews 3:12) and the miracle took place. Surrounded as I was by chatting, smoking men and women, I was healed, first spiritually and then physically." Yet there was no sudden, sensational change in Babsie's outward condition.

For weeks, even months, she had to "fight the good fight of

faith" (1 Tim. 6:12). Again and again Babsie would say to me, "The old enemy is just round the corner (for she knew only too well the signs of the coming migraine attack) but the Lord has given me a word" (Matt. 4:4). I saw, lived out before me, the power of that word (Psalm 107:20) for, every time that Babsie leaned her whole weight upon the promise of God, she found healing maintained. Seven years have passed since that unforgettable moment in the train, and the healing taken by naked faith has become a permanent reality.

The Lord truly gave me a new wife. It was great to labour with a fellow-worker upon whose ministry the seal of God rested, and who was so obviously enjoying God-given health. The healing stood the test of fifteen months of continuous convention work in Britain; a return visit to Australia, when we preached in churches of various denominations and took part in three Keswick conventions; eight months of ceaseless travelling in Japan; four months in tropical Singapore.

And now once more we are back in our homeland. I am writing this in the library of the A.E.B. Bible College, where my wife is serving the Lord as Matron, and where I have the privilege of lecturing to the students.

Alice is here too, having returned with us from Japan, after helping Neil and Peggy for twenty months in their Headquarters near the City of Osaka. We are, however, praying that she may be led back to Japan, as a Spirit-filled missionary.

Our son is living here in Cape Town, a few miles from us. He is married to Dawn Hatton, a lovely girl whom he met at the Bible College, and they are expecting their first baby in November. Reginald has completed his theological course, and is now the "Rev. R. P. Friend".

He is at present working with the Scripture Union but may, if the Lord so leads, accept a call to a church.

Babsie and I are, however, still "gipsies". God willing, we shall be going next year to Britain for nine months of convention work, but hope to return to the A.E.B. Bible College, if the Master tarries. After that? What? We know not!

"Peace, perfect peace, our future all unknown,
Jesus we know, and He is on the Throne."

We are encompassed about with uncertainty, but of one thing we are sure: As we move in the will of God, our Immanuel will be with us, "every one of the days, even to the very end."